Hosanna!

Blessed Frederic Ozanam: Family and Friends

Rev Ronald Ramson, CM

WestBow
PRESS
A DIVISION OF THOMAS NELSON

WestBow Press books may be ordered through booksellers or by contacting:

WestBow Press
A Division of Thomas Nelson
1663 Liberty Drive
Bloomington, IN 47403
www.westbowpress.com
1-(866) 928-1240

Because of the dynamic nature of the Internet, any web addresses or links contained in this book may have changed since publication and may no longer be valid. The views expressed in this work are solely those of the author and do not necessarily reflect the views of the publisher, and the publisher hereby disclaims any responsibility for them.

Cover image courtesy of The Association of the Miraculous Medal, Perryville, Missouri. The artist Gary Schumer captures the life of Frederic Ozanam who appears in his academic robe as he ministers to the poor.

ISBN: 978-1-4497-9680-8 (sc)
ISBN: 978-1-4497-9681-5 (hc)
ISBN: 978-1-4497-9683-9 (e)

Library of Congress Control Number: 2013909590

Printed in the United States of America.

WestBow Press rev. date: 07/11/2013

Frederic Ozanam's life program:
"to become better, to do a little good"[1]

1   Sacra Congregatio pro Causis Sanctorum: Frederic Ozanam, Positio Super
     Virtutibus. Informatio et Summarium, Rome, 1990, pp. X1V-XV

Hosanna:[2]
Hebrew: "save" or "rescue"
In classic Hebrew: "please save" or "save now"
A cry of joyful praise or adoration
A family name

---

2   *Hosanna* is a Hebrew word derived from the words *yasha*, which means to "save," and *na*, an expression of request and can be translated in a variety of ways. In Hebrew, the word appears as *Hoshana*.

Definitions can be found in the 1913 Catholic Encyclopedia article on Hosanna and the Encyclopedia Britannica, Eleventh Edition, a publication now in the public domain.

Contents

Preface

His mother called him Deric; he called her Maman. She signed her letters to him Mme. Oza. His father was Papa; his father called him Fred. His two brothers were Alp and Charles.

The ecclesial world knows him as Blessed Antoine-Frederic Ozanam.

His wife, Amelie, was the first love of his life among other first loves. In his letters to her, Amelie was *ma chere amie* or *chere bien-aimee*; publicly, he called her his guardian angel. Amelie also often referred to him as Fred. Their daughter Marie was the apple of his eye.

His father-in-law was not Jean-Baptiste, but Father. His mother-in-law was not Zelie, but Mother.

In Frederic's life, the poor took center stage next to Jesus Christ.

His students in the lecture hall of the prestigious Sorbonne, Paris, called him "professeur," admired and respected for the person of integrity that he was.

The professional world knew him, in modern parlance, as an academic rock star, scholar, colleague, author, and that rare combination of brilliant intellectual and saint.

Countless persons—Lyonnais, Parisian, and foreign—called him friend. He signed his correspondence to them "A.-F. Ozanam."

The bishop of Nimes, Claude-Henri Agustin Plantier, called him "The angel of charity, the athlete of faith."

Others refer to him as Apostle of Truth and Apostle of Charity. Blessed John Paul II referred to him as the Precursor of Social Justice.

Worldwide members of the Society of Saint Vincent de Paul know him as their principal founder. To Frederic, they were his confreres.

I call him Frederic, rarely Ozanam, because he is my friend and inspiration.

All these personal synonyms and accolades for a man who lived but forty years!

Introduction

Why a book on Frederic Ozanam? I read somewhere that people do not write biographies of others unless they know that the person was far above the ordinary. Frederic's brothers must have felt the same way, as they both wrote biographies of him. And so did several others, including the renowned Pere Henri-Dominique Lacordaire, OP, and the distinguished Kathleen O'Meara, Msgr. Louis Baunard, and Albert Paul Schimberg.

Why am I writing a biography of Frederic Ozanam? Because he is far above the ordinary and because, I believe, he has something to say in word and action to today's world. Lacordaire said, "Ozanam: that type of Christian, as ancient as his religion, as modern as his time." I would say, "As modern as today."[3]

Frederic Ozanam experienced a world of upheaval, economic disaster, social injustice, horrendous poverty, and epidemic diseases, and yet he lived through it all happily and successfully. Frederic speaks to single and married, students and professors, and professionals and volunteers.

Frederic was a remarkable lover of his wife, child, family, the poor, his collegians and colleagues, and his God. He exemplifies the person in whom faith and action meet, in whom intelligence and holiness shine. He was a man who discovered the secret of how to balance it all.

Why this biography? To provide updated information in English regarding Frederic Ozanam's life and family that is not

---

3   Positio, op. cit., p. vi. Lacordaire may have borrowed his comment on Ozanam from Saint Augustine's *The Confessions*: *"Late have I loved you, O Beauty, ever ancient, ever new"* (Book X, 27, 38). The Confessions, translated by Maria Boulding, O.S.B., Vintage Books, New York, 1998.

available except in French. The sorry fact is that even the French has had a limited circulation, which I hope in time will be rectified.

Frederic Ozanam saw the risen Christ in the other—a gift that many would die for. And do.

Acknowledgments

I have known Antoine-Frederic Ozanam in thought, word, and deed for fifty years. We are old friends.

What have been the sources of my knowledge of him? It is impossible to cite them all; books, articles, workshops, and magazine pieces primarily in French, Spanish, and English. I have "relived" Frederic's life in various locations; for example, in his beloved French cities of Lyon, Paris, and Dax and in Burgos, Spain. These locations have provided me with wondrous experiential knowledge of the man. I cannot overlook prayer because he and I have been and still are "in conversation." We have talked often, especially when I have felt a pressing need.

Over the years, I have come to feel that I, in some spiritual way, have gotten to know the Ozanam family. I have seen their positive more than their negative side, their virtues rather than their vices. I sense that I have not been intruding but have been welcomed into their circle—that they have been eager to reveal themselves and have wanted to share their lives. Still, what I have discovered is how much of Frederic Ozanam's life I do not know. He has hooked me and entices me to dig deeper into his life, but as I have done so, I realize how much more there is to this incredible human being. "You duped me, and I let myself be duped" (Jeremiah 20:7).

This biography is lean; I have trimmed the fat, omitted speculation and assumptions, and revealed current information, much of which was not available in earlier biographies.

My main thrust in *Hosanna! Blessed Frederic Ozanam: Family and Friends* is friendship since that was a hallmark of his life and apostolate. Amazingly, for a man we might well classify as rather introverted, Frederic had a huge gallery of friends that he maintained contact with until his death, a fact to which his vast correspondence testifies.

Besides the knowledge I have accrued over the years, I have focused on two main sources: *Disquisitio de Vita et Actuositate Servi Dei*—the tome presented to the Sacred Congregation for the Causes of Saints in 1980 for the beatification and canonization of Frederic Ozanam—and the five volumes of *Lettres de Frederic Ozanam* published over the years in France. I thank the Superior General of the Congregation of the Mission, G. Gregory Gay, C.M., for permission to quote from the *Disquisitio*. I am grateful to the International President of The Society of Saint Vincent de Paul, Dr. Michael Thio, for permission to quote from the letters of Ozanam.

I found these sources to be more reliable and accurate. There will be a few noticeable discrepancies in these works in comparison to earlier biographical materials, some of which, I suspect, have depended more upon previous materials than on independent investigation. I have personally translated much of the French materials, but not exclusively.

I want to thank Mr. Roger Playwin, Executive Director of the National Council of the Society of St. Vincent de Paul of the United States, for permission to quote from "Frederic Ozanam: A Life in Letters," translated and edited by Joseph I. Dirvin, C.M.

I thank the Association of the Miraculous Medal, Perryville, Missouri, for permission to use Mr. Gary Schumer's painting of Frederic Ozanam for the cover.

All quotes and references from Sacred Scripture are taken from The New Testament, Revised Standard Version, Liturgical Press, Collegeville, Minnesota.

Family

*Parents, Siblings, Wife,
and Daughter*

The family is the privileged setting where every person learns to give and receive love.

The family is itself based primarily on a deep, interpersonal relationship between husband and wife, sustained by affection and mutual understanding.

The family is a necessary good for peoples, an indispensable foundation for society, and a great and lifelong treasure for couples.

Together with passing on the faith and love of God, one of the greatest responsibilities of families is that of training free and responsible persons.

The Christian family is called the domestic church because the family manifests and lives out the communal and familiar nature of the church as the family of God.

Parents, in virtue of their participation in the fatherhood of God, have the first responsibility for the education of their children, and they are the first heralds of the faith for them. They have the duty to love and respect their children as persons and as children of God ... in particular, they have the mission of educating their children in the Christian faith.

The family is also a school which enables men and women to grow to the full measure of their humanity. The experience of being loved by their parents helps children to become aware of their dignity as children.

Grandparents ... are so important for every family. They can be—and so often are—the guarantors of the affection and tenderness which every human being needs to give and receive.[4]

---

4   The Fifth World Meeting of Families, 8 July 2006, Valencia, Spain

The Ozanam Family Tree[5]

Grandparents of Antoine-Frederic Ozanam:

Benoit "Pierre" Ozanam (1729–1800) + Elisabeth Baudin (1736–1803)

Parents of Antoine-Frederic Ozanam:

Jean-Antoine Ozanam (1773–1837) + Marie Mariette Nantas (1781–1839)
Married 22/4/1800, Lyon, France

Children of Ozanam and Nantas:

Elizabeth Eliza Ozanam (1801–1820)
Jeanne-Caroline Ozanam (1802–1802)
Charles-Alphonse Ozanam (1804–1888)
Marie-Caroline Ozanam (1811–1812)
Non Prenommee Ozanam (1814–1814)
Amelie-Caroline Ozanam (1814–1814)
Amelie Ozanam (1816–1816)
Charles-Auguste Ozanam (1818–1819)
Non Prenommee Ozanam 1819
Pierrette-Adelaide Ozanam (1820–1820)
Louise-Marie-Helene Ozanam (1820–1820)
Louis-Benoit Ozanam (1822–1822)
Charles Ozanam (1824–1890)

---

5 Sacra Congregatio pro Causis Sanctorum Frederici Ozanam. Beatificationis et canonizationis servi Dei Frederici Ozanam. Disquisitio, Rome, 1990, pp. 15-17

Only surviving children:

Charles-Alphonse Ozanam: medical doctor, priest, and monsignor
Antoine-Frederic Ozanam: lawyer, professor of foreign literature, and author
Charles Ozanam: allopathic doctor and homeopath, surgeon, and researcher

What's in a Name?

What's in a family name? History. What does it say? Volumes.

In 1805, Jean-Antoine-Francois Ozanam wrote that his family was of Jewish origin. Jeremie Hosanham, a praetor in the Roman troops, served under Julius Caesar in the seventh legion. The story goes that Jeremie was awarded a sizeable tract of land by Caesar in compensation for his military expertise as displayed in the Gallic wars. This provides a plausible reason how a Jewish colony sprang up in the area known as Bouligneux.

In the 1879 biography of his brother Frederic, Msgr. Alphonse Ozanam comments on his father's earlier writings and states that "our family was Jewish in origin as the name indicates." The monsignor surmises that the family name was originally written "Hozanna."[6] This seems closer to reality than not. It was not uncommon in earlier times for individuals to spell their names differently, sometimes in the same manuscript. Today, we observe the correct and exact spelling of our last names, forced to do so because of legal requirements and strict identification purposes.

In the year 607, Saint Didier, then archbishop of Vienne, fleeing persecution of Queen Brunehaut (whose scandalous life the archbishop had openly criticized), stopped in a place called

---

6   Disquisitio, op. cit., p. 7 Also, the Jewish roots are mentioned by Dr. Antoine Ozanam in his "Livre de famille" (1805), by Msgr. Charles-Alphonse Ozanam in his biography of his brother Frederic (1879), and by Frederic Ozanam himself in a letter to Alexander Ferriny-Jerusqlemy, #1286, 6 May 1853, San Jacopo, Italy. All quotations from Ozanam's correspondence can be found in one of the five volumes of his letters written from 1819 to 1853: *Lettres de Frederic Ozanam* commissioned by The Society of St. Vincent de Paul, Paris, France. These letters in French serve as the main source of Frederic Ozanam's ideas and ideals. *Frederic Ozanam: A Life in Letters* translated and edited by Joseph I. Dirvin, C.M. also has been an excellent resource for materials.

Bouligneux where he was welcomed in the home of Samuel Hosanham. Didier converted him and his family to Christianity and baptized them in the month of July.

Unfortunately, soon afterward, the queen's henchmen—actually her sons—captured Didier and strangled him to death on the banks of a stream called Renom. A village is now located near the spot, Saint Didier de Renom. The present-day citizens refer to themselves as "Desideriens" and "Desideriennes" after Saint Desiderius, or Saint Didier.

It was Jean-Antoine's father, Pierre Benoit, born in Bouligneux, the family homestead, who changed the spelling of the family name to what we know today, Ozanam.

The Would-Be Father

Jean-Antoine-Francois Ozanam, the future father of Antoine-Frederic Ozanam, was born in Chalamont in Dombes, France, 19 July 1773, the oldest and sole survivor of four children of Pierre Benoit and Elisabeth Baudin. He began formal schooling at the age of ten in Bourg-en-Bresse and finished there in August 1790.

Jean-Antoine studied philosophy for two years at the seminary of Saint Irenaeus, Lyon, aggregated with the University of Valence. When the seminary faculty refused to comply with the government's edict of taking the required civil oath, the seminary closed in 1791.

Benoit wanted his son to be a magistrate. He placed Jean-Antoine as an intern with the legal registrar of Bourg-en-Bresse, and when there was an opening, he was chosen for the similar civil position at Pont-d'Ain. However, before he was able to assume the post, he was drafted into military service.

In October, his first stint was with the Eighth Artillery battalion of Ain, and in November 1793, he joined the hussar regiment of Benchiny, a fast-moving, hard-hitting light cavalry. Jean-Antoine actively engaged in Napoleon Bonaparte's Italian campaign and, as a consequence, in the course of four battles was wounded five times, three rather seriously.

After almost seven years of active duty, at twenty-six years of age, Jean-Antoine left the hussars with the rank of captain—not merely because of his physical scars but also because of his disagreement with Bonaparte's political shift from republic to empire. The change was too drastic for a patriotic soldier of the republic.

Love and Marriage Go Together Like...

Jean-Antoine opted for the municipality of Lyon to seek employment. He found a job working on commission with a company called Dantoine, which he soon left.

According to civil records, he married Marie Nantas on 20 April 1800; he was twenty-six, and she was nineteen. Her parents were Mathieu Nantas and Marthe-Etiennette Richard. Mathieu welcomed his new son-in-law into the silk industry of Lyon. Things looked more than promising!

Unfortunately, Jean-Antoine lost his father, Pierre Benoit Ozanam, on 27 November 1800, eight months after his marriage began. In 1801, he and Marie decided to move to Paris, and this time, he became associated with the Haraneder brothers. The older brother, Louis, had married Marie's sister, Benoite. Jean-Antoine was working for the extended family.

Although the new Ozanam family was doing well, there were storm clouds on the horizon—the price of warfare was making things unstable in the financial world. After two years of association with the Haraneder brothers' firm, the war with England occasioned bankruptcies everywhere. The Haraneders lost their company and fortune—four hundred thousand francs. They had to liquidate and dissolve their firm.

Jean-Antoine tells us in his journal that these days were the unhappiest of his life. He lost his mother on 21 March 1803; his youngest sister-in-law, a teenager named Annette Nantas, died 14 February 1803; his wife's uncle, whom they loved very much; and, above all, he says, they lost "our fortune." All this in 1803! Not a good year to say the least.

We cannot overlook the Haraneders who lost everything as well. Jean-Antoine's sister-in-law, Benoite, found herself and her family in the same dire straits as her sister, Marie Ozanam.

Jean-Antoine Hits the Road

Besides losing everything, including all their furniture, there were two other mouths to feed. Jean-Antoine and Marie were parents of two children: Elisabeth Eliza, born 13 February 1803 in Lyon, and Charles-Alphonse, born 6 January 1804 in Paris. Eliza's birth was the only bright spot in 1803.

Jean-Antoine had one thing in mind: the care and support of his family. There was never any doubt, given his personality and military history, that Jean-Antoine would ever back down from a challenge or not try anything and everything to put food on the table.

What to do? One of the first possibilities was the resumption of his military career. With his reputation and excellent record, he would have been easily accepted back into the hussars, but he decided against it. In collaboration with a Mr. Varilla, husband of his wife's cousin, they established a freight depot for French merchandise at the Italian port of Livorno. Before leaving for Livorno at the end of 1807, Jean-Antoine settled his wife, daughter, and son in Lyon in the suburb of Saint-Irenee. Here they stayed until May 1809. However, the freight business in Livorno had a short life. The port was closed in February 1808 because of political issues.

The job search continued. Jean-Antoine moved to Naples for business opportunities, but after some serious threats by the English, he left that city for Milan.

Interestingly, his son Frederic would later draw from his father's many varied work experiences when he spoke on social justice issues.

A New Start: Milan, Italy

Jean-Antoine was a married man with children, living a bachelor life. He hoped for a new life with his family, but they were still back in Lyon. He sent for Marie and the two children—Elisa, now age six, and Alphonse, age three. They arrived in Milan in July 1809. They had not seen each other in almost two years.

The family rented lodging with the Ladies Bonnet, originally from Lyon, whom Jean-Antoine knew well. Thanks to them, he soon got a job: the translation into French of a sizable legal document, which paid him handsomely.

As Jean-Antoine never flinched from any possible job, he undertook teaching mathematics. He was a man always in search of something better. The family found new housing, and here he created a small boarding school, which soon became quite popular. He taught math, French, Latin, and Italian, which he spoke very well, as one can only imagine after his many job experiences in Italy. Everyone in the household worked for their bread and butter.

Marie Ozanam handled the physical upkeep of the house, aided by their faithful servant, Marie Cruziat, who came with Marie from Lyon.

Marie Ozanam used her skill in sewing dresses for the upper-class, stylish Milanese women that provided some supplementary income. She was determined to help her family stay together and recoup their stability. Marie only stopped dressmaking when Jean-Antoine opened a small school for young men, an addition to the boarding school. Jean-Antoine kept the boarding school going from 1809 to October 1816; it succeeded beyond their expectations.

Jean-Antoine found his definitive vocation: medicine. Stability had come. What a difference a vocation makes!

Doctor Ozanam, MD

How advantageous it is to have family and friends who know you and feel free to make specific suggestions for your welfare!

A celebrated surgeon of Lyon, Marc-Antoine Petit, a close relative of Marie Ozanam, came to Milan at the request of a Mr. Blondel to perform a cataract operation. While there, Dr. Petit suggested to Jean-Antoine that he seriously consider the medical profession. But Dr. Petit did more. He personally introduced Jean-Antoine to the renowned professor and medical author Dr. Antonio Scarpa and to other influential persons. As a consequence, the doors of medicine were flung open, and he matriculated at the University of Pavia as a student.

Jean-Antoine tells us that he copied notes of the professors lent to him by several excellent students in the class. These men were no doubt younger and took the older and amiable classmate under their wings. It could have been that his military reputation greatly impressed them.

Jean-Antoine worked sixteen hours a day on his medical studies and on lessons for the boarding school students. Here was a working medical student! Another incredible fact: Jean-Antoine walked to and fro the university—twenty-three miles one way!

During the school's holidays, June to November 1810, Jean-Antoine reviewed the professors' lectures with his six student friends whom he saw as strengthening boosters for his studies. In December 1810, Jean-Antoine passed his exams at the University of Pavia, receiving his doctor of medicine degree on 27 December 1810 "a pieni voti e con laude." The government minister exempted him from practice (probably a type of internship). Jean-Antoine was now free to exercise medicine throughout the entire kingdom of Italy, that is, the northeast part of the country.

Doctor Ozanam immediately went to work in the hospitals of Milan. With the retreat of the Russians, the wounded Italians, French, and Austrians appeared on the scene. He treated everyone. Then an epidemic of typhoid ravaged the country. He showed his zeal although he had limited resources. In recognition of his services, Jean-Antoine was decorated with the Order of the Royal Crown of Italy on 8 April 1814.

Thanks to his priest son Alphonse, we have a vivid description of his father's view of medicine. Jean-Antoine had bounced from one job to another and from one city to another but always in pursuit of a good-paying job for his family. But here we see a different man. Alphonse writes, "Medicine was, in his eyes, a species of priesthood, and he would repeat that idea often, for in fulfilling its functions with dignity, it was necessary to be disposed to give his life to the sick if circumstances would render the necessary sacrifice."[7] Alphonse had at least two good examples to back up his father's words: the doctor's work with the victims of the typhoid epidemic in Milan and with the victims of the riots of November 1831 in Lyon and again in 1834. The priest's words were prophetic. Doctor Ozanam did give his life for the poor sick as a result of a serious fall he suffered because of poor lighting in a tenement house in Lyon.

There is another dimension to this remarkable man. Doctor Ozanam was also an author, writing on the subject of silk so significant to the economy of the city of Lyon and on the field of medicine and chemistry. His major accomplishment, the one he is known for with a very long title, was "The General Medical History of Contagious Diseases Which Reigned in Europe from Remote Times and Notably from the Fourteenth Century to Our Days."[8]

---

7   Disquisitio, op. cit., p. 23

8   Author's translation of Dr. Ozanam's text

The five-volume work was published first in 1817. In 1835, Jean-Antoine reissued a new edition condensed in four volumes with additional material on cholera morbus, which was beginning to penetrate Europe. There was another edition in 1840 published after the doctor's death.

Frederic was quite proud of his father. As a student of the Sorbonne in Paris, he wrote his mother and asked her to say something flattering to Papa because Professor Gabriel Andral, chair of general pathology on the faculty of medicine of Paris, spent almost the entire class on the work of his father (the history of epidemics) and cited nothing but the highest praise of the work.

Dr. Ozanam held positions of doyen of medicine at Hotel Dieu Hospital and enjoyed memberships on various medical societies of Lyon, Brussels, Palermo, and others. He was a highly regarded medical doctor by his colleagues and patients.

Patriotism Trumps

Up to this point in history, Milan was under jurisdiction of the French government, but with the treaties of 1815 and the move of the Austrians into Lombardy, there was no way that Doctor Ozanam was going to remain in Milan. He packed up the family and moved back to Lyon. Here was a true Frenchman who loved his country and had almost died several times in defense of it. He refused to live and work in an area no longer under French jurisdiction.

More about His Mother

Marie Nantas's marriage with Jean-Antoine Francois Ozanam was a mixture of the best and worst of life during their first sixteen years together. During the beginning years of married life, Marie became acquainted with the perks of luxury, but after the whole bottom fell out through bankruptcy, she discovered the life of poverty. Not surprisingly, she handled it extremely well. The cream surfaced, and she showed heroic courage. She was not afraid to get her hands dirty for the good of her marriage and family.

Marie was born 15 July 1781; her husband's birthday was four days later. She was the third child of Mathieu and Marthe-Etiennette Nantas. Marie knew the fine things of life because her father was a successful silk merchant, and the family was considerably well off. Mathieu later became administrator of Hotel Dieu, the general hospital of Lyon.

The Nantas had three other children: Benoite, Jean-Baptiste, and Annette. Benoit was born in 1774; she married the elder of the Haraneder brothers, Louis. It was they who started a company called Pyrenees Atlantiques in which Jean-Antoine Ozanam became an employee shortly after his marriage to Marie.

Jean-Baptiste was born between his two sisters Benoite and Annette. Annette followed their brother in 1786 but died at the early age of seventeen.

While Jean-Antoine knew war from the outside looking in, Marie knew revolution from the inside looking out. She and the Nantas family were quite familiar with the horrors of the Great Terror in Lyon by the military of the Convention. The family hid in the cellars of the building while the troops were circulating on the Lyonnais streets above.

The reign of terror was exactly that. We will never know how many people were killed. The official count runs at twelve thousand, but many others were shot, drowned, or put to death in some other horrific way. The favorite method was the guillotine. The terror was supposed to help the revolution survive, but too many of the common people were executed to justify the brutality and violence. Incidentally, 674 clergy were guillotined.

Mr. and Mrs. Nantas and son Jean-Baptiste were arrested at the beginning of October 1793 but released. All the family possessions were illegally confiscated. At age nineteen, Jean-Baptiste was among the fatal victims of 3-4 December 1793 gunfire in Brotteaux Square. The Nantas family were devastated over the loss of their only son.

The Nantas family decided to make their escape and found refuge in Switzerland at the small village of Echallens in the region of Vaud near Lausanne. It was here in a small church that held services for Catholics and Protestants that Marie Nantas made her first communion. She never forgot that moment and often shared her memories with the family.

The Reign of Terror ceased 28 July 1794. When calm had been restored in France, Mathieu took his family back home to Lyon. They had to make a new start.

Marie's future son Frederic will take his family to Echallens in June 1847 and relive his mother's days there. Frederic reminisces,

> I paid a visit to the church where my dear mother made her First Communion … it was as my mother described it, divided into two parts, one for Catholics and one for Protestant worship. The dear church is very badly kept, yet I prayed in it with more fervor than usual. I thanked God for all the favors he had bestowed in this same place on the exiles. I prayed for my dear mother only because it is a

duty to pray for the dead. As I believe that she is happy and powerful in heaven, I asked her to watch over us, to help us to conclude safely this long drawn-out journey, and above all to obtain for her children some of her sweet virtues. My wife and my mother-in-law prayed with me, and my darling Marie knelt quite seriously at the altar rail.[9]

There are several striking things about the Ozanam and Nantas families: their ability to live through the most difficult situations, to suffer significant losses in goods and family members, the resiliency to bounce back and begin all over again whenever needed, and their patriotism for France, specifically their love for Lyon that we see throughout Frederic Ozanam's life and relationships.

---

9   Disquisitio, op. cit., "Notes de voyage," 21 June 1847, p. 22-23

Mrs. Ozanam Back in Lyon

Even after Jean-Antoine's attainment of doctor of medicine, Mrs. Ozanam, who had had a solid and practical education, made her own clothes, supported her husband in any way possible, and oversaw the homeschooling of the children with admirable attentiveness.

Marie was an active member in the Church of Saint-Pierre. She belonged to a group of women called Societe des Veilleuses (literally, Society of Watchers). It was composed of poor working women who alternately took turns sitting all night with women who were ill or indigent. Marie Ozanam was a take-charge type; she grouped thirty of the "Watchers" to give them instructions and maintain the zeal necessary for such a task. Imagine sitting up all night with someone who is ill surrounded by the worst living conditions!

Frederic Ozanam learned the secret of visiting poor families by accompanying his mother through the streets of Saint-Pierre parish. He knew the poor years before his personal involvement as a member of the Society of Saint Vincent de Paul.

Guigui

Doctor Ozanam had said that the year 1803 had been among the unhappiest of his life, but what about June 1820? That may have been a month or a year that he well wanted to forget. Besides his pressing medical practice, his wife was highly weakened because she had just given birth to twins who were in critical condition, their seven-year-old son Frederic had come down with the deadly typhoid fever, and there were two other children to care for. All this was going on simultaneously. How could he manage it all by himself? He couldn't, and he didn't. He had expert help; her name was Maria Cruziat.

We would probably think of Maria Cruziat in terms of a maid or a housekeeper, and she was all that, but much more. Maria Cruziat was family.

The children called her Guigui. Why? Why do kids often come up with names for loved ones out of nowhere or for reasons that existed for a fleeting moment in time but then got lost in space? Even in their adult years, to the Ozanams, Maria was usually called Guigui or affectionately referred to as Old Maria. At a critical time in his life Frederic asked for prayers from "my good Guigui."[10]

Guigui was born at Priay (Ain) near Chalamont where Doctor Ozanam was born. She entered the service of his paternal parents in 1785 at the age of seventeen and went to work at the home of Jean-Antoine and Marie Ozanam during the height of their financial problems. She accompanied them to Paris, Milan, and Lyon. Guigui was a fascinating woman who, when the Frederic Ozanam story is told, is unfortunately minimized, but she was the Ozanam's rock of Gibraltar. She was shrewd in handling finances

---

10   Letter, #1268, Charles Ozanam, 29 March 1853, Pisa, Italy

and adhering to a household budget and a person the Ozanams always consulted in family and personal decisions, although lacking a formal education, she held a degree in street-smarts.

At the death of Marie Ozanam in 1839, Guigui stayed with the three brothers, Alphonse, Frederic, and Charles, at the homestead in Lyon. She accompanied the three when they reunited in Paris and moved in with Frederic and Amelie in October 1843. When Frederic died in 1853, she moved into Charles's home where she lived out the last four years of her life. In a letter of 1 July 1845, Frederic mentions that Guigui had been serving the fourth generation of Ozanams.

Guigui was a woman of fidelity; she was in the service of the Ozanams for seventy-two years! She never had a job description. She sometimes traveled with the Ozanam family to help with the children, prayed countless rosaries for the family members, and sung the same French lullabies to three generations of babies. Each child born in any Ozanam household felt the same love and affection from Guigui that their parent had known as a child.

From One to Four

Over a period of twenty-three years, Doctor Jean-Antoine and Marie Ozanam were the parents of fourteen children, five sons and nine daughters, of which only three sons survived.

Their first child was Elisabeth, whom they called Eliza. She was born in Lyon, 13 February 1801. Eliza lived through most of her teens until 1820. Doctor Ozanam wrote in his journal that although Eliza had a frail constitution, she never had been bedridden. She came down with a light fever but grew worse, finally expiring on Thursday, 29 November at 1:30 in the morning.

Eliza had been the guardian angel of her younger siblings, beloved of her mother as the firstborn of her parents' love, and was the apple of her father's eye. As the two oldest, Father Alphonse tells us that his father encouraged his sister and him to maximize their skills.

The girl displayed extraordinary talent. She had a genuine facility in languages, especially English, was excellent in drawing and painting, and loved to dance. Her father was one of her greatest supporters in the field of music because of his own musical abilities; he could play the violin, clarinet, and horn.

Frederic identifies that it was Eliza, his beloved sister, who collaborated with his mother in homeschooling and whom he thoroughly enjoyed. Frederic took her death very hard. He lost not only his teacher and sister, but also his best friend.

The next Ozanam born was also a girl, Jeanne-Caroline. The place was Paris; the date 24 June 1802. She died less than two months after birth on 3 August from convulsions.

Charles-Alphonse, the oldest of the three survivors of the

Ozanam children, was also born in Paris on 6 January 1804. He had an interesting vocation and lived to be eighty-four.

Marie-Caroline was born in Milan on 16 December 1811 and died at the beginning of January 1812.

Antoine-Frederic

The fifth born of the Ozanams and the subject of this biography was Antoine-Jean-Frederic, born at 11:00 p.m. on 23 April 1813 in Milan. A plaque commemorates the occasion:[11]

Antonio Federico Ozanam
nacqve in qvesta casa il XXIII Aprile MDCCCXIII

Antoine-Frederic was baptized 13 May 1813 in the parish of Santa-Maria dei Servi; his godfather was Antoine Michel and godmother was Claudia Bonet.

Doctor Ozanam tells us that it was in June 1820 that Frederic contracted typhoid. He was seven years and three months old. The doctor called it "putrid fever." Typhoid is a contagious continual fever that lasts from two to three weeks. It is now considered nonfatal, but that was not the case during the Ozanam's time.

Doctor Ozanam, a man who was quite an expert on contagious diseases, was helpless, as he could do nothing for his ailing child. In spite of her pregnancy, Marie spent hours on end at her son's bedside, doing whatever she could to make the boy as comfortable as possible. Her experience with the sick poor as a Watcher came in handy.

The Ozanams pinned a relic of Saint Jean-Francois Regis to Frederic's pajamas. They prayed to the saint for his intercession for their son's survival and recovery from certain death. The French saint who had dedicated his life to the poor was a favorite of the two bewildered parents. Did they know that Jean-Francois had been canonized the same day in June 1737 as Saint Vincent de

---

11   The plaque is fixed to Frederic Ozanam's birthplace in Milan, Italy.

Paul? They will come to know much about this latter saint in future years.

Ten years later, Frederic wrote,

> At seven years old I had a serious illness, which brought me so near to death that everybody said that I was saved by a miracle; not that I lacked kind care: my father and mother hardly left my bedside for fifteen days and nights. I was on the point of expiring when suddenly I asked for some beer. I had disliked beer, but it saved me. I recovered.[12]

Frederic may have asked for a beer in his delirium from the high fever. From the seventeen- year-old's writings, he seems to be rather cavalier about the episode. A beer didn't save him; it was a miracle. The vast majority did not survive from typhoid. The better approach would give credit to the intercession of Saint Jean-Francois Regis and the praying Doctor and Mrs. Ozanam. And we can't forget the ever-present Guigui. God had special plans for the young seven-year-old who would later become Blessed Frederic Ozanam.

Frederic's brother Alphonse wrote that Frederic's "life was in danger from the moment of his birth."[13]

Frederic's health would be viewed as delicate or fragile as evidenced throughout his life: the typhoid fever scare, whooping cough (twice), and susceptibility to colds, respiratory elements, pleurisy, and finally Bright's disease.

---

12   Letter, #12, Auguste Materne, 5 June 1830, Lyon

13   Disquisitio, op. cit., p.1064

Numbers Six to Fourteen

The Ozanams gave birth to twins: Amelie-Caroline and Ann-Angele on 21 June 1814. One of the girls died after birth, the other fifteen days later.

The eighth child, Marie-Amelie-Stephanie, was born in Milan on 19 February 1816, but she died three weeks later of erysipelas ("Saint Anthony's Fire") after the family had moved back to Lyon on 26 November 1816.

Charles-Auguste, who was born on 24 February 1818, died of convulsions and dysentery eleven months after birth on 29 January 1819 in Fontaines-sur-Saone, a village close to Lyon.

A daughter, born dead on 1 June 1819, was the Ozanam's tenth child. Her first name is unknown.

Marie Ozanam gave birth to another set of twin daughters on 16 June 1820 in the midst of her son Frederic's bout with typhoid fever. The girls were Louise-Marie Helene and Pierrette-Adelaide. Pierrette died ten days later and Louise on 13 August. As June 16 is one of the feast days for Saint Jean-Francois Regis, it would be interesting to know when the doctor and his wife pinned the saint's relic to Frederic's pajamas and what part the saint played in the safe delivery of the twin girls.

The Ozanam's thirteenth child, Louis-Benoit, was born on 19 March 1822, the Feast of Saint Joseph, but died at three months on June 20 from smallpox—or more probably from diarrhea and convulsions—at the village of Brindas, close to Lyon.

The last child, another boy, was named Charles, born in Lyon on 31 December 1824. He would survive and outlive his two brothers Alphonse and Frederic and die in 1890.

How difficult it is to witness the death of a child, the fruit of one's love. But Doctor Jean-Antoine and Marie Ozanam experienced the death of eleven children! What does this say about these two people? Their determination never faltered, their faith was unfathomable, and their love for each other defeated any loss and sorrow.

Today, they would be highly criticized for their actions from various camps, possibly hearing "They should have ceased having kids years before" or other statements. If they had stopped, would we have the man Blessed Antoine-Frederic Ozanam and be commemorating his life?

Frederic wrote years later about his parents,

> On many occasions have I not seen my parents in tears; when heaven had left them, but three children out of fourteen! But how often, too, have not those three survivors, in adversity and in trial, counted on the assistance of those brothers and sisters whom they had among the angels! ... and are brought back to our minds in acts of unexpected assistance. Happy is the home that can count one half of its members in heaven to help the rest among the narrow way which leads there![14]

Here are words appropriate to explaining the practical ramifications of the communion of saints. We thank Frederic for his thoughts.

Who knows the impact of the deaths of their brothers and sisters on the three Ozanam brothers? Is this one of the reasons why Frederic had such compassion and sensitivity toward family, friends, and the poor? No doubt he learned to love those in poverty by the example set by his mother and father.

---

14   Letter, #1056, Joseph de Champagny on the death of his child, 14 February 1851, Paris.

Charles-Alphonse Ozanam

Charles-Alphonse Ozanam was born 6 February 1804 in Paris, France, and died on 26 November 1888 in Paris at the age of eighty-four. He was called Alp by the family, the oldest of the three surviving Ozanam children. What emerges from even a cursory reading of Alphonse's life is that he was a man who seemed to have lacked stability and flickered from one place to another. Was this due partly to the turmoil of the time, or was it due mainly to his personality? Or a combination of both? These are questions for discussion. From what we read in correspondence, there are no critical comments from the family. Alphonse was Alphonse, a man admired and loved. However, others labeled him as "difficult, anxious, and very unstable."[15]

Alphonse tells us that his father greatly encouraged his skills in music because his father also was a gifted musician. Alphonse played the violin at the early age of five or six and with some expertise. His father, a former hussar, taught him how to ride a horse.

It seems that Alphonse's name appears on the list of "Good Works" on 17 April 1825. This means that he became involved with Emmanuel Bailly, who would play a big part in the life and ministry of Alphonse's brother Frederic Ozanam. Alphonse was lodging on a street close to the school of medicine.

In 1826 at twenty-two years old, Alphonse became a medical doctor like his father. Within four years, Archbishop de Quelen of Paris ordained Alphonse as a subdeacon and then as a deacon in Notre Dame in 1830. At twenty-seven years old, on 26 February

---

15 Disquisitio, op. cit., p.1066

1831, he was ordained a priest for the archdiocese of Lyon where he first served as a hospital chaplain and then a parochial vicar.

Doctor Ozanam talks about his newly ordained priest son in the concluding months of 1831. It appears that Father Ozanam was serving as a hospital chaplain at two hospitals. The priest found himself spending most of his time caring for wounded men who were without assistance. He exposed himself to grave danger whenever he had to pass through the mob on the way to minister spiritual and temporal assistance to the misfortunate. From Charity Hospital Alphonse went to Hotel de Ville to administer to the wounded.

Having been wounded himself five times, three times rather severely, during his time in the military, the Doctor was quite proud of his son's attention to the wounded of the Canut uprising even though it posed some danger for him.

The next venture for Alphonse was as a member of a diocesan group, missionaries of Chartreux of Lyon (1835–1841). This group lived in a community established in the ancient chartreuse of the Croix-Rousse area of Lyon. The community ministered to the silk workers—the Canuts—who lived in the tenements and worked in the area, a scene of various uprisings over inhuman working conditions. These revolts began in 1831 and ended in 1870, the date of the decline of the silk industry due to foreign competition and the emergence of synthetic silk.

With a certain amount of that Ozanam pride, Frederic refers to his brother at least six times in his letters as a missionary priest of Chartreux. Alphonse's membership in the Society of Mary (Marist) followed from 1841–1846. He was dispensed from vows in 1847. Incidentally, Alphonse was a Marist when he performed the marriage ceremony for his brother Frederic.

After the dispensation from vows in the Marist Community, Alphonse took an administrative position at College Stanislas in

31

Paris from 1846—1847, but was dismissed from the school in the middle of October 1847 for reasons that are not clear. It does seem, however, that the archbishop of Paris was included in the mix.

According to records, Alphonse was incardinated into the archdiocese of Paris in 1850, yet in the first half of January 1848, he was obliged by the archbishop to accept a chaplaincy at the military hospital at Lille where he retained his ministry from 1848–1850. Alphonse is next seen in the Parisian Church of Saint-Merri, a small church on the right bank as parochial vicar for Father Jean-Louis Gabriel, a canon of Notre Dame. Alphonse held that ministry for five years.

Alphonse moved to the Church of Saint-Germain-des-Pres in 1855, the oldest church on the left bank. He entered retirement in 1860 and situated himself first at Saint Cloud, now a western suburb of Paris, when he was fifty-six years old. He resided the remaining days of his life in Paris where he died in 1888, five years after completing a biography of his brother Frederic.

That is quite a journey for any priest and says much about his personality and eighty-four years of life. There is no indication that Alphonse was anything but a good priest.

Alphonse officially witnessed the marriage of his brother Frederic to Amelie on 23 June 1841. Their brother Charles, age seventeen, served the Mass.

The three Ozanam brothers had a deep affection, respect, and concern for each other. At age twenty-three, Frederic went hiking in Switzerland with Alphonse. Frederic said that his big brother had to get away, as he was doing missionary work in the archdiocese of Lyon and, in his little brother's estimation, was under a lot of stress from his priestly responsibilities. It also afforded them the opportunity to get away from the political turmoil of France. Frederic described the beautiful nature they saw and how he thoroughly enjoyed their being together.

Previous to Frederic's wedding, Alphonse was visiting Charles, their teenaged brother. Frederic writes to Charles,

> How I have wished to change places with you for a while these past few days and to visit for some hours with Alphonse, whom I see in my mind's eye ... with that stubborn disease of the knee ... in choosing God's service, he has chosen the best part. Despite his troubles, is he not still the guide and consoler of others? He is especially mine at this time.[16]

A year later, Frederic writes that he has begged for "our dear Alphonse the graces his ministry has need of, the definite reestablishment of his health so long uncertain and the joy of soul, recompense of a life vowed to good." Frederic prayed for "that fraternal union, symbol of and prelude to the heavenly company of the saints" and that "we shall be united in the same meeting place; our mother will be there too."[17]

Alphonse had served as a parochial vicar from 30 April 1850 at Saint-Merri in Paris under Abbe Marie Gabriel, who concluded his ministry as pastor in 1866. The abbé was a former chaplain of the military hospital in Lyon. It is quite possible that Father Ozanam got to know Abbé Gabriel while both were fulfilling their priestly responsibilities in Lyon. It is not clear if the abbé sought out Alphonse for his associate or if Alphonse requested a position from the abbé.

Alphonse and Charles were but a letter away when Frederic needed them. When the ship docked at the port of Marseilles with Frederic's dying body aboard, the two brothers were there and remained with him during his final hours. Alphonse recited

---

16   Letter, #314 Charles Ozanam, 19 May 1841, Paris

17   Letter, #387 Charles Ozanam, 28 March 1842, Paris

the prayers of the dying as he had done for their mother fourteen years before. At the funeral Masses in Marseilles, Lyon, and Paris, they were there.

Monsignor Alphonse Ozanam was buried in Paris at the Church of Saint-Sulpice in 1888.

One last thought: One theory of recent years is that Father Alphonse Ozanam introduced his brother Frederic to the lay apostolate in the world in 1835. This theory is not found in any of the earlier biographies of Frederic Ozanam and needs further exploration. A supportive argument to the theory could be that the Society of Saint Vincent de Paul was founded by lay people, is governed by lay people, and did not and does not involve church administration as such. This was quite different from Blessed Pope Pius XI's Catholic Action that appeared on the scene later.

Charles Ozanam[18]

Charles Ozanam 1824–1890 + Anne-Lise D'Aquin 1834–1907
Married 10 September 1855 Ile-de-France, Paris, France

Children:

Alphonse Ozanam 1856–1933
Marie Ozanam 1859–1933
Therese Ozanam 1861–1933
Frederic Ozanam 1862–1941
Maurice Ozanam 1864–
Elisabeth Ozanam 1866–1880
Jean, Martin, Joseph Ozanam 1868–1930
Francois Ozanam 1870–1949
Joseph Ozanam 1872–1919
Marguerite Ozanam 1874–1944
Madeleine Ozanam 1876–1968

---

18 Charles Ozanam's genealogy is found on-line in French and English.

Charles Ozanam

Charles was called "Charles" by the family; no nickname, except in a letter to his mother, Frederic referred to his seven-year old brother as "Charlot": "he hoped no longer has the fever."[19]

Charles ended up much like an orphan in Lyon after the deaths of his parents within two years of each other. After all, Charles was only halfway through his teen years when they died and was still attending secondary school. Alphonse and Frederic were gone out of the house, and the Ozanam homestead remained. Who took care of it? Who took care of Charles? Guigui, of course. The rock. Charles could not have been in better hands. Remember, Guigui was family!

Frederic was delighted with his younger brother when Charles joined the Society of Saint Vincent de Paul. He wrote to Charles,

> Let us thank divine providence for having brought us both to enter this young and growing family which may be destined to regenerate France ... Souls are returning to the faith; it grows slowly like things that last and will continue ... as long as we do not compromise it by our weakness or imprudence. The more seriously you enter into your studies, the better you must perceive the higher light of religion sheds upon them which nothing can replace.[20]

We hear Frederic's concern for his young brother in these words. Frederic and his wife, Amelie, had attended Mass at Notre Dame in Paris about which he wrote,

---

19   Letter, #45, to his mother, 8 April 1832, Paris

20   Letter, # 496 Charles Ozanam, 25 June 1843, Nogent-sur-Marne

I could not forget my brothers. I asked wisdom for you (Charles) which reinforces judgment, that strength which sustains the will amid the thunderstorms of adolescence. I have asked that you may preserve that piety with which you are endowed, so that you may know your vocation and will not fail in the courage to follow it.[21]

Charles found his vocation and the courage to follow it: the vocation of his father, medicine. He did his internship from 1846 at three hospitals in Lyon, one being Hotel-Dieu where his father had led a distinguished career, Enfants Malades, and Sainte-Marguerite.[22] Charles received his degree in medicine on 28 December 1849.

Charles became involved in homeopathy. It appears that various members of the Ozanam family and friends were homeopathic practitioners, including Frederic.[23] A London-based homeopath report[24] states that Frederic, his wife Amelie, and daughter Marie contracted whooping cough in 1847 and that Frederic almost died.

While Doctor Jean-Antoine Ozanam had written a well-received work on contagious diseases, Charles wrote a good number of articles for medical journals. He was a colleague of a few celebrated French medical personalities, such as Paul Francois Curie, Pierre Jousset, Jean Paul Tessier, and others in the field of homeopathy.

Two years after Frederic's death, Charles married Anne Lise D'Aquin on 10 September 1855 in Paris. Anne was born and

---

21   Letter, #387 Charles Ozanam, 28 March 1842, Paris

22   Letter, #703 Alphonse Ozanam, 23 December 1846, Florence, footnote #154

23   Letter, #1225, Charles Ozanam, 19 January 1853, Pisa, Italy

24   Sue Young Homeopathy, website of a London based homeopath, comments on Charles Ozanam who became a doctor of homeopathy.

raised in New Orleans, Louisiana, and was ten years younger than Charles. She died in Paris at the age of seventy-two on 8 September 1907, the anniversary of Frederic Ozanam's death.

Anne and Charles were the parents of eleven children, the exact number of his siblings who had died in childhood: Alphonse Francois Eugene, Marie Pauline Marguerite Amelie, Louise Marie Therese, Frederic Joseph Eugene, Maurice Joseph, Elisabeth, Jean Marius Joseph, Francois, Charles Pierre Joseph, Marguerite Marie Eugenie, and Marie Madeleine.

Their daughter Marie Pauline Marguerite Amelie took vows in a religious community, their son Jean Marius Joseph became a medical doctor like his father and grandfather, and their son Charles Pierre Joseph was ordained to the priesthood like his uncle Alphonse, but, unfortunately, he died at the age of forty-seven. All the siblings died in France, except Francois who died in Manitoba, Canada, at the age of seventy-nine.

In 1862, Pope Gregory XVI bestowed on Charles the distinguished Order of Saint Gregory the Great in recognition of his service to the church, of unusual work in support of the Holy See, and a good example.

Charles passed away in Paris on 11 February 1890 at sixty-five, two years after his brother Alphonse.

Charles was another example of Ozanam ancestry—men and women who traditionally gave their lives in service for others whether in church, science, higher education, or government.

Antoine-Frederic Ozanam
and Amelie Soulacroix

Antoine-Frederic Ozanam 1813–1853 + Marie-Josephine-Amelie Soulacroix 1821–1894

Married 23 June 1841, Church of Saint Nizier, Lyon, France

Child of Ozanam and Soulacroix:

Marie-Josephine Ozanam 1845–1912

Priest or Husband? That Is the Question

Frederic Ozanam was in the midst of discernment and had been for some time: priesthood or marriage?

His parents were both deceased. He judged that he owed at least one year's mourning to the memory of "my poor mother" who died in 1839. In the meantime, he was praying for the grace of decision. "I invite all my friends to help me with their prayers in these grave and decisive circumstances.[25]

The one who was most anxious for Frederic's answer was Father Henri Lacordaire who had switched from diocesan priesthood to the Dominicans and wanted Frederic to join him in reestablishing the Dominican community in Paris. Lacordaire was looking for quality, and he saw it in the person of Antoine-Frederic Ozanam—intellectual brilliance and solid spirituality. Frederic muses, "I shall see the Abbé Lacordaire on his return from Rome" and "assure myself whether divine providence may not be willing to open to me the doors of the order of Saint Dominic." In the meantime, his plan was "to win some little claim to fuller lights from above, by acquiring more austere habits and greater control over my passions that I might have more certainty of being actuated by the right intention."[26]

The discerner was the priest who knew Frederic from his earliest teens and probably better than anyone—not his spiritual director, but his long-time mentor Abbé Noirot. Frederic opened his heart and got an answer from his mentor, "Get married, *mon cher*, get married."[27]

---

25   Letter, #227, Henri Passoneaux, 13 March 1840, Lyon

26   Ibid.

27   Frederic Ozanam: His Life and Works, Kathleen O'Meara, New York Christian Press Association Publishing Co., New York, 1911, p. 133

Noirot, the sage and professor of philosophy, had always had the unwavering opinion that Frederic never had a vocation for the religious life. He was a man in need of tenderness, compassion, and encouragement, all of which Noirot thought that Frederic would receive in marriage, particularly from the right young woman. The wise man had someone very specific in mind and became a matchmaker.

That Girl…

Was it a setup or not? Years later, Frederic attributed it to divine providence. He wrote his fiancée, "The more the beloved figure comes near bathed in clearer light, the happier I am with the choice providence has made for me."[28]

Frederic had an appointment to see Mr. Jean-Joseph (called Jean-Baptiste) Soulacroix, the rector of the Academy of Lyon. As Frederic moved from one room to another, he noticed a young woman caring for an invalid named Theophile, the brother of the attractive girl, Amelie. Did she notice Frederic? He certainly noticed her, as all during his conversation with Soulacroix, his eyes shifted her way. Abbé Noirot's hopes were fulfilled; Frederic had been hooked. It would be only a matter of time.

The couple was formally engaged on 9 January 1841.

---

28   Letter, #280, Amelie Soulacroix, 24 January 1841, Paris. Frederic mentions this two weeks after his formal engagement to his fiancée Amelie.

Amelie: Love at First Sight...

Who was she? Her name was Marie-Josephine-Amelie Soulacroix, who was born in the bustling port city of Marseilles in 1821. At that time, her father was a professor of mathematics at the Royal College.

Soulacroix is an interesting name. Literally, it means "under the cross."[29] As a single, young woman, Amelie lived under the cross of her brother's illness; in marriage, she would live under the cross of the unforeseen illness of her husband.

Amelie and Frederic started dating. It grew serious, and they were formally engaged. As a sign of their love and affection, they exchanged identical lockets that contained snippets of their respective hair, which they wore until death.

About six weeks before their wedding, Frederic panicked. He had a custom of kissing the locket before going to sleep. For whatever reason, he decided to open the locket one night to gaze at the snippet of Amelie's hair and found it missing, as the clasp had broken. Frederic searched his room for a good solid hour without any luck. He could not find his fiancée's hair!

The next morning, Frederic was a mixture of sadness and embarrassment. He sat down and wrote a letter to Amelie, who was back in Lyon, and told her the truth. The letter is a clever composition that evokes the imagination and rings with the dramatic and the poetic. Frederic asked Amelie not to cut off another ringlet but to send him one from her mother's scrapbook.

A great amount of time during their engagement was spent apart, as Amelie was in Lyon, and Frederic was in Paris. There was no e-mail, cell phones, or fax machines. Only postal mail. Frederic

---

29   The author's interpretation of the family's proper name

wrote Amelie long letters, telling her what was happening, but more than just informational, for many were tender love letters. He wrote twenty-nine letters to her while she was his fiancée and sixty to her as his wife.

Frederic was a lover. He loved God, he loved his profession as professor, he loved the poor with whom he ministered as a member of the Society of Saint Vincent de Paul, and he was madly in love with Amelie Soulacroix. He did not hesitate to put his feelings down in black and white. Amelie would answer his letters, for which he anxiously awaited. Distance does make the heart grow fonder. Frederic's first letter was written to Amelie 22 December 1840 and the letters never stopped coming.

Frederic wrote Francois Lallier in December,

> I have recourse to your prayers. May God preserve, during this exile of six months, her whom he seems to have chosen for me, and whose smile is the first sunbeam of happiness that has brightened my life since my poor father's death. You will find me very tenderly smitten. I don't try to disguise it, although sometimes I cannot help laughing at myself! I believed my heart was more bronzed ...[30]

During much of their engagement, Frederic was confronted with a major decision: teach at Lyon or at the Sorbonne in Paris? Frederic wanted Amelie's input.

Should they remain at Lyon? He could offer her more material comfort, the close association with their families and friends, and greater certainty and security. The salary for the position Frederic was offered as chair of foreign literature in the University of Lyon would be nearly six times of what they could expect at the Sorbonne. The alternative was a low salary and the prospect of poverty but

---

30   Letter, #265, Francois Lallier, 6 December 1840, Lyon

a vast field of possibilities at the prestigious Sorbonne, his alma mater, and life in the capital of France with all its promise.

Amelie put her hand into Frederic's. "I trust you. It's Paris."[31]

In the end, it is whether the man and woman are best friends.

---

31   O'Meara, op. cit., p. 142

Wedding Bells

The big day had come. It was Wednesday, ten o'clock in the morning, in the Church of Saint-Nizier, the downtown area of Lyon. In attendance was Father Joseph Mathias Noirot, matchmaker of the soon-to-be newlyweds. He was also one of the signees as an official witness of the marriage. Also attending the happy occasion were many of the Soulacroix family, Mr. and Mrs. Pierre Jaillard, Christophe Falconnet, Joseph-Alexandre Bedel, the Haraneders, and a good number of others, including members of the Society of Saint Vincent de Paul.

Frederic described his emotions. He was on his knees. At the altar was his eldest brother, Alphonse, p.M,[32] and his teenaged brother Charles, who was serving the Mass. At his side was the young girl Amelie dressed in white and veiled, pious as an angel, who already gave him the tender and affectionate feeling of a friend. Surrounded by her parents, she was even happier than Frederic, whose parents were deceased. But he did have his two brothers, some friends, and "confreres"[33] of the Society. The church was full, and all were deeply moved by the ceremony.

Frederic did not know where he was. He could scarcely restrain his huge, delicious tears as he felt God's blessing descending on Amelie and himself "with the consecrated words." In a letter to Francois Lallier, who could not make the wedding, Frederic wrote soon afterward, "I let myself be happy. I take no account of hours or moments. The lapse of time is nothing to me. What do I care

---

32   At this time of his life, Father Alphonse Ozanam belonged to the Society of Mary (Marists). The religious community originated in Lyon, France, in 1816.

33   In France, members of the Society of St. Vincent de Paul are referred to as "confreres"; in other countries of the world, as in the United States, they are called "Vincentians."

about the future? Happiness is in the present—it is eternity ... I understand heaven." Here is a man in love! Frederic added, "Each day, in revealing to me new perfections in her whom I possess, increases my debt to providence ... what a difference from those days when you saw me so sad in Paris."[34] He told another close friend, Jean-Jacques Ampere,

> My happiness is great; it surpasses all my hopes and dreams. Since the day that the benediction of God descended on me, I am dwelling in a sort of enchanted calm. So serene, so sweet, that nothing can give an idea of it. The angel who is come to me clothed in every grace and virtue is like a new revelation of providence in my obscure and laborious destiny; I am illuminated with interior joy. [35]

The honeymoon was long. They started in France but spent most of their time in Italy. Frederic said, "The journey was like an enchanted dream." [36]They were both fascinated by the scenery and history of Sicily, and Rome made an indelible impression on them.

A highlight of the trip was meeting Pope Gregory XVI.[37] He and his young bride had a private audience with his Holiness. Frederic wrote:

> He spoke to me of France...of my studies. I received his blessing for me, for my family, for the Society of St. Vincent de Paul with which he was acquainted and which he loved.[38]

---

34   Letter, #331, Francois Lallier, 28 June 1841, Chateau du Vernay, pres Lyon

35   Letter, #330, Jean-Jacques Ampere, 26 June 1841, Chateau du Vernay, pres Lyon

36   O'Meara, op. cit., p.144

37   Pope Gregory XVI's pontificate ran 1830 to 1846.

38   Letter, #365, Henri Pessonneaux, 12 November 1841, Paris. Also, Disqusitio, op. cit., p.304

The twenty-third of every month, the anniversary of their marriage, Frederic gifted his wife with flowers.[39] He never forgot and made sure that she received flowers even on his deathbed. Sometimes he also presented her with a poem that expressed his love for her. Shortly before he died, Frederic wrote his "guardian angel," as he called Amelie, a love poem that was to be given to her after his death.

Amelie was always on Frederic's mind.

After Frederic's death, Amelie wrote:

> Having spent two-thirds of my life in the intimacy of this indeed remarkable man, this saint, and this good friend, I feel the need of still living by his memory and all that is connected with his memory that is dear to me.[40]

The Society of St. Vincent de Paul was approved by the Holy See: Disqusitio, op. cit., p.305.

39   Disquisitio, op.cit., p.590

40   Ibid., op. cit., pp.1005-1006

An American Connection: In-laws

Frederic Ozanam's father- and mother-in-law were Jean-Joseph (usually referred to as Jean-Baptiste) and Zelie Soulacroix, whose maiden name was Magagnos. Her parents were Joseph Magagnos and Rose-Josephine Magagnos (a cousin). They married on 11 May 1799 at Norfolk, Virginia. Joseph was listed as a captain. They had two daughters: Zelie, born 1798 in Norfolk, and Adele, born 1794 also in Norfolk.

Interestingly, various public legal documents list names of the Magagnos family, e.g., the parish court index of Norfolk, Virginia records, the Free African-Americans for Borough of Norfolk, Virginia (free Negroes residing in the borough as of 1 February 1836), etc. The Magagnos were very much a part of Norfolk scene; they owned property and at least one business. Three Magagnos were co-owners of a leather shop in Norfolk.

Zelie Magagnos married Jean-Joseph Soulacroix on 10 November 1819 in Marseille, France. Their daughter Amelie, who married Frederic Ozanam, was born on 14 August 1821 in Marseille also.

Not only was Zelie an American, but Charles Ozanam's wife was as well.

Marriage: Frederic's Insights

From our experience, the best marriages are between husbands and wives who are best friends.

In his book *Civilization of the Fifth Century* in the chapter entitled "Christian Women," Frederic describes marriage as follows:

> In marriage there is not only a contract, there is, above all, a sacrifice, a twofold sacrifice. The woman sacrifices that which God has given her, and which is irreparable, that which was the object of her mother's anxious care—her fresh, young beauty, often her health, and that faculty of loving which women have but once.
>
> The man, in his turn, sacrifices the liberty of his youth, those incomparable years which never return, that power of devoting himself to her he loves, which is only to be found at the outset of his life, and that effort of a first love to secure to her a proud and happy lot. This is what a man can do but once, between the ages of twenty and thirty ...
>
> This is why I say that Christian marriage is a double sacrifice. It is two cups; one filled with virtue, purity, innocence; the other with an untainted love, self-devotion, the immortal consecration of the man to her ... who was unknown to him yesterday, and with whom today he is content to spend the remainder of his life; and these two cups must both be full to the brim, in order that the union may be holy, and that heaven may bless it.[41]

---

41 Civilisation au 5me siècle, Frederic Ozanam, Les Femmes Christiennes, Vol. II, p. 97; quoted in length also in O'Meara, op. cit., p.189.

The Joy of Fatherhood

Amelie and Frederic wanted a family. Amelie had at least two miscarriages in three years. Frederic expressed his concern to friends over his beloved wife's physical condition each time, but on 24 July 1845, after four years of marriage, he was ecstatic with joy, exclaiming to his friend Theophile Foisset,

> After so many favors that were set down in my vocation in this world, a new blessing has come to me, to know the greatest joy probably it is possible to experience here below: I am a father!
>
> We prayed much; we begged for prayers on every side; never did we feel greater need of the divine assistance! We have been heard above and beyond all hopes. Ah! what a moment that was when I heard the first cry of my child; when I beheld that little creature, but that immortal creature, which God has confided in my hands, who brought me so many delights and also so many obligations!
>
> With what impatience I waited for the moment of her baptism! We have given her the name Marie, which was my mother's name, and in memory of the powerful patroness to whose intercession we attribute this happy birth. We will begin her education early, and, at the same time, she will begin ours; because I perceive that heaven has sent her to us to teach us a great deal, and to make us better.

How could I dare teach her lessons that I did not practice? Could God have found a kinder way of instructing me, of correcting me, and setting my feet on the road to heaven?

There is nothing more delicious on this earth than on coming home to find my beloved wife with her baby in her arms. I then make a third figure in the group, and I would willingly lose myself for whole hours in admiring it, if presently a little cry did not come to warn me that poor human nature is very fragile … and the joys of fatherhood are only given us to sweeten its duties.[42]

As usual, Frederic's thoughts are unusual.

Father Alphonse Ozanam performed Marie's baptism. Amelie's mother, Zelie Soulacroix, was godmother, and Francois Lallier was the godfather. There were three generations of the family present: father Frederic, grandfather Jean-Baptiste, and great-grandfather Joseph Magagnos.

For Frederic's mother, Assumption was her special day, which the entire family celebrated while she was alive, but it was also the day after Amelie's birthday. Frederic designated the Assumption as the special day for his daughter as well. One time, when on vacation in London, Frederic sent Marie a letter on 14 August to wish her a happy feast and to remind her that it was a great feast of the Holy Virgin also.

I am asking her to pray for you so that you are very wise and that the Good God love you.

Pray also for your papa and for your mama, who very much miss kissing you today. I will try to make a good feast for

---

42   Letter, #636, Theophile Foisset, 7 August 1845, Paris

your mama. I am now coming back from buying her flowers, and I am going to take her to a store where she will choose a dress. But she would very much prefer a kiss from little Marie.[43]

Frederic tells Marie to wish Guigui a happy feast and to thank Uncle Alphonse for the earrings he bought for her. "Embrace with your whole heart your grandma who is good to take care of you ... and I bless you as your beloved father." [44]

Marie was eight when her father died on 8 September 1853 in Marseille, the city of her mother's birth. Amelie was a young thirty-two.

Before Amelie died at age seventy-three, she was blessed to see her daughter's wedding and to enjoy grandchildren. Marie Ozanam married Laurent Laporte at the Church of Saint-Sulpice in Paris on 16 July 1866. They had but one son, Frederic, who married a young lady named Marguerite Recamier.

Frederic Laport, Ozanam's grandson, had seven children neither his grandson or great-grandchildren ever met him: Gabrielle 1898-1980; Sabine 1900-1998; Marie, who lived to be 101 and died in 2003; Francois who was born in 1907, ordained to the priesthood, and died in 1983; Jean was born in 1909 and was killed in 1942 during World War II; Magalie 1910-1999; and Frederic who died at birth in 1913.

---

43   Letter, #1098, Marie Ozanam, 14 August 1851, London
44   Ibid.

Marie Ozanam and Laurent Laporte

Marie-Josephine Ozanam 1845–1912 + Laurent Laporte 1843–1922

> Married 16 July 1866, Church of Saint-Sulpice, Paris, France

Child

> Frederic Laporte 1868–1922

Frederic Laporte

Frederic-Claude-Marie Laporte 1868–1922 + Marguerite-Anne-Marie Recamier 1877–1951

Married 9 July 1896, Ile-de-France, France

Children of Laporte-Recamier:

Gabrielle Laporte 1898–1980
Sabine Laporte 1900–1998
Marie Laporte 1902–2003
Francois Laporte 1907–1985
Jean Laporte 1909–1942
Magali Laporte 1911–1999
Frederic Laporte 1913

Marie Ozanam

Pregnancy had not been easy for Amelie Ozanam. Frederic wrote Abbé Marc-Antoine Soulacroix that "from the end of November (1844) Amelie was condemned by the doctors to absolute rest".[45] Previously, she had had miscarriages, and the doctors opted on the side of extreme caution.

On Thursday morning, 24 July 1845, Frederic dashed off two letters, one to Adele Haraneder and the other to Francois Lallier. "I want to thank God. God has made me a father. This morning at five o'clock, after three hours pain that ended with a happy delivery, my poor wife gave me a little daughter" (combined thought). Frederic was overjoyed.

Frederic and Amelie named their girl Marie in memory of his mother and the Blessed Virgin Mary "in memory of the powerful intercession of whom we attribute this happy birth."[46]

The proud father was pleased that Marie's baptism was celebrated with solemnity by his brother, Father Alphonse Ozanam. His mother-in-law, Zelie Soulacroix, was godmother, and Francois Lallier was godfather. Three generations were present for the occasion: Frederic, grandfather Jean-Baptiste Soulacroix, and great-grandfather Joseph Magagnos.

That little daughter Marie was indeed the apple of her father's eye. Frederic sometimes referred to her by the nickname "Nini," but it is usually restricted only to his brothers, Alphonse and Charles. He spent quality time with her and was determined to direct her

---

45   Letter, #632, Abbe Marc-Antoine Soulacroix in Belgium, 31 July 1845, Paris

46   Letter, #636, Theophile Foisset, 7 August 1845, Paris. It should be noted that "Marie" was the first name of Amelie Ozanam as well: Marie-Josephine-Amelie Soulacroix Ozanam.

education himself as soon as she was able. He remembered how he had loved his sister Eliza, his first schoolteacher.

Frederic wanted Marie to share his love of the poor, which he had learned from his own mother and father. He wrote Marie's godfather, Francois Lallier, that after Christmas Mass, he took the two-year-old Marie with him to visit the homes of the poor, and that she had given some of her toys to the children in the families, which pleased Frederic to no end.[47]

When Frederic died on 8 September 1853 in Marseille, Marie was eight years old. Her mother Amelie was thirty-two and, incidentally, never remarried. Amelie saw that her primary responsibility was the growth and education of their daughter and spent her time and energy caring for the love of her life. Amelie and Marie went frequently to the crypt of the chapel where Frederic was buried, where they took bouquets of flowers.

Amelie struck up a close friendship with Jeanne Adelaide Recamier, the wife of her doctor. Jeanne had been a widow with four children when she met and married the famous doctor, Joseph-Claude Recamier, who also had been married previously.

Joseph-Claude Recamier was chief physician at Hôtel-Dieu in Paris and professor on the faculty of medicine at the College of France. He is credited with the popularization of several instruments in gynecological medicine.

Mrs. Recamier often invited Amelie and Marie to her home, which was lively with a good number of children. Both also spent time at the home of Leon Cornudet, a member of the Society of Saint Vincent de Paul, a man who had been a close friend of the deceased Frederic Ozanam.

Because women were not yet included as members in the Society of Saint Vincent de Paul, Amelie, who had practiced the sacrificial acts of mercy toward her infirm husband Frederic,

---

47   Letter, #775, Francois Lallier, 31 December 1847, Paris

since his death, channeled her mercy toward other individuals and projects. She was no longer worried about the raising and educating of Marie, as she was mature and responsible. Amelie has been credited with organizing the first subscription for Peter's Pence and later assisting Cardinal Charles Lavigerie, founder of the Missionaries of Africa, in his foundations.

Marie Ozanam was quite attractive at eighteen. She met Laurent Laporte from Lyon at one of the social gatherings at the Recamiers; he was in law school. They fell in love and were married in the Church of Saint-Sulpice on 16 July 1866, eight days before her twenty-first birthday. Amelie was blessed to see her daughter's wedding day and the birth of her grandson, Frederic Laporte.

Amelie got into a routine social schedule: Wednesday dinner at the Laporte's, Saturday at the Recamier's, and Sunday at her house with family and friends.

During the siege of Paris in 1870–1871, Amelie and her mother, Zelie Soulacroix, fled to Ecully near Lyon at the invitation of the Laporte family who owned property there. Amelie's home in Paris had been taken over by the "Federes" ("les communards") and trashed.

Amelie noticed that her grandson Frederic, who was twenty-six, was quite taken with the seventeen-year-old daughter of General Max Recamier, Marguerite. Amelie did not have the joy of seeing this marriage because she died at seventy-three on 26 September 1894 at Ecully, two years before their marriage. She was buried in Montparnasse cemetery next to her parents and her young brother Theophile.

A word about Frederic and Amelie's grandson Frederic Laporte.

Frederic Laporte and Marguerite-Marie Recamier were married in 1896. They had seven children. Gabrielle, the firstborn, married Paul Montariol. Sabine married Heni Houssay, and Marie lived to be 101 and died in 2003. Francois was an ordained priest and a member of the Sulpicians, who left the Society of Saint-Sulpice in 1944, joined the Mission de France in 1955, and died in 1983. Jean married Magdelaine Lesca and died in 1942 at thirty-three during World War II. Magdali married Frederic Bremard. And Frederic, surely named after his father and grandfather, died at birth in 1913.

Frederic Ozanam would have been proud of his grandson Frederic Laporte, who was brilliant like his grandfather. Grandson Frederic was an alumnus of Ecole Polytechnique and graduated from the School of Mines, Paris. He became a pioneer in the field of electricity, authored several scientific articles, and delivered presentations in key cities of Europe. He was chosen to represent France at an international meeting at Washington, DC in 1910, and played a major role there at the Bureau of Standards in collaboration with scholars from the United States, England, and Germany. He was unanimously selected by his colleagues to present the final committee report.

Frederic did extensive research for the French navy on submarines. When World War I broke out, he joined the military service and held the position of artillery captain in 1914. However, while on the battlefield caring for his men, he developed a cardiac problem. Authorities took him out of active combat and placed him as an artillery instructor at Fontainebleau. After military discharge, Frederic continued research on submarine batteries for the French navy.

Frederic was granted the Legion of Honor in January 1918 by the French government for his military services. Failing health forced him to retire in March 1922. He died at the age of fifty-four on 17 July in the same year. His wife Marguerite lived until 1951.

Frederic's Friends

Close and Closer

A Friend: The Best Medicine in Life

"Faithful friends are a sturdy shelter; whoever finds one has found a treasure. Faithful friends are beyond price; no amount can balance their worth. Faithful friends are life-saving medicine" (Sirach 6:14–16).

Aelred of Rievaulx, in his famous work *Spiritual Friendship*, says that "the best medicine for life is a friend."[48] "In every action, in every pursuit, in certainty, in doubt, in every event and fortune of whatever sort, in private and in public, in every deliberation, at home and abroad, everywhere friendship is found to be appreciated, a friend a necessity, a friend's service a thing of utility."[49]

Tullius states, "Friends though absent are present, though poor are rich, though weak are strong, and though dead are alive."[50]

In the gospel story of the paralytic, his friends carry the man to Jesus and lower him through the roof of the house. They are clever, creative friends—life-saving medicine—the best medicine. Seeing their faith, Jesus heals the paralytic.

How often do our friends carry us to God? How important is it to cultivate good friends? Such friends help sustain us in our friendship with God and with each other and deepen that respective friendship. We know where bad friendship can lead us!

---

48 Aelfred of Rievaulx: The Way of Friendship, introduced and edited M. Basil Pennington, New City Press, Hyde Park, N.Y., Book 2:13, p.63

49 Ibid., op. cit., p.63

50 Cicero (106-43 BC), *Laelius De Amicitia*, Loeb Classical Library, Book 7, 23, p.134, 1923. (Text is in public domain)

Friendship Is

The ultimate criterion for friendship is this: "No one has greater love than this, to lay down one's life for one's friends" (John 15:12–13). This has to be the most demanding standard of friendship!

Who of us does not long for intimate, prolonged, and mature friendship? Friends are one of life's greatest gifts—precious possessions—treasures. Philosophers have described friendship as a "single soul in two bodies," or speak of a friend as "a second self."[51]

The key to friendship is self-disclosure. We open up our mind and heart and let the other inside. Any relationship is only as good as its communication. Authentic friends share the totality of self—joys and sorrows, hopes and fears—and do it because they trust each other.

Friends bring out the best in us and vice versa. They accentuate the positive and minimize the negative. Friends know our dark side and show their compassion in bearing with it.

Friends do damage control. Friends, even the closest, cause hurt. Friendship can be a roller coaster ride at an amusement park. Unfortunately, our mouth gets in the way and out pops a word or phrase that should have remained inside. Friendships often display a sign that reads "Under Repair." Although they are treasures housed in earthen vessels, friendships are not necessarily fragile when genuine.

Friendship is stronger than death because its bond is love. Love does not cease with death. The letter to the Hebrews reminds us of "the great cloud of witnesses"[52] who are on the sidelines rooting us toward eternal life.

---

51 Such phrases are found in a number of classical texts by Aristotle, Cicero, and Aelfred of Rievaulx to name but three.

52 Hebrews 11:2

Like love, friendship is free; it is not bought or sold. We select friends freely, and the challenge is to select cautiously and wisely. What we discover in life is that we become our friends, for better or for worse. Take a look at our gestures, for example. From where have some come? Look at the gestures of our friends.

Saint Paul says it well, "Rejoice with those who rejoice, weep with those who weep" (Romans 12:15). That is what we do in friendship. We celebrate, we lament.

Friendship: The Least of Love and...

C. S. Lewis says in *The Four Loves*, "Friendship is the least natural of loves; the least instinctive, organic, biological, gregarious and necessary. It has least commerce with our nerves, there is nothing throaty about it; nothing that quickens the pulse or turns you red and pale."[53]

Friendship is built on a common commitment or shared interest in something that is good and true. It cannot be forced, pursued, or won. As Lewis writes, "The very condition of having friends is that we should want something else besides friends ... Friendship must be about something."[54]

In Book VIII and Book IX of his work *Nicomachean Ethics*, Aristotle gives us an in-depth coverage of friendship. He concludes that a friendship will persevere only in the measure that two friends fall in love, not so much with each other, but together with a transcendent third. For example, if the two look with love toward one of the transcendentals of being, such as unity, truth, goodness, and beauty or perhaps toward their nation or the city in which they live. This is looking with love toward a transcendent third. But what if that transcendent third is God? Do the two then look with love toward the Transcendent?

These thoughts connect us back to the two foundational principles of friendship in Frederic Ozanam's life. Was God the transcendental third for Frederic, the service of truth, patriotism, the good works of charity—one or all of these—or something in addition?

The first and last word on friendship is "No longer do I call you servants ... I have called you friends" (John 15:15).

---

53   The Four Loves, C.S. Lewis, Harcourt, Inc., Orlando, 1960, p.58

54   Ibid., op. cit., p.66

Frederic Ozanam and Friendship

In the mind and heart of Blessed Frederic Ozanam, friendship flowed from two foundational principles: one from his patron and inspiration, Saint Vincent de Paul, and the other from his own lived experience.

> "Seek God alone, and he will provide us with friends and with everything else, so much so that we will lack nothing."[55]

> "The strongest bond, the principle of a true friendship is charity, and charity cannot exist in the heart of many without pouring one's heart outward. It is a fire that dies without food, and the food of charity ... good works."[56]

These two principles were actualized in the life of Frederic Ozanam through the combined efforts of his private and communal prayer, his vast correspondence, and communication in interpersonal relationships, in the lecture hall, in the public arena, and in the homes of the destitute.

A phenomenon prevalent in the lives of the saints is their propensity to surround themselves with companions of intelligence, integrity, and deep faith. Such persons were mutual friends.

With whom do we surround ourselves? Do we have friends like the paralytic?

During the last year of his life, Frederic wrote to a friend,

---

55 Vincent de Paul: Correspondence, Conferences, Documents, Vol. 11, Letter 23, p.31, New City Press, Hyde Park, New York, 2008

56 Letter, #82, Leonce Curnier, 4 November 1834, Lyon

Charles Lenormant, "I still don't know what God will demand of us, but he certainly has done enough for the honor and pleasure of our life in the choice of friends ... he has made me acquainted with the greatest Christians of my time and souls of the best choices."[57]

57   Letter, #1223, Charles Lenormant, 12 January 1853, Pisa

The Poor

The poor were Frederic Ozanan's friends; he loved them. Ozanam's home visits to the poor played a dominant part in his life. He had such a sensitive heart that he was unable to be indifferent to their suffering.[58] He saw service to the poor as a service of love. His manner toward the poor was always one of serious concern and differential; he considered himself an equal among equals, never superior to them, although intellectually he was a giant among the ordinary. Frederic made the words of Saint Paul his own:

> Be of the same mind, having the same love, being in full accord and of one mind. Do nothing from selfish ambition or conceit, but in humility regard others as better than yourselves.[59]

When he entered a home, his immediate words were: "I am your servant", something you could expect from someone who viewed his ministry with the poor as a service of love.[60] He never put down anyone; he thoroughly enjoyed talking to people, even those classified as illiterate and crude. He listened and offered words of consolation and advice.

Here was a person who loved the poor; they were indeed his friends. Above all, in the mind of Frederic Ozanam, they were the Risen Jesus made visible.

---

58   Disquisitio, op. cit., p. 1071
59   Philippians 2: 2-3; see also Romans 12:3
60   Disquisitio, op.cit., p.1071

Andre-Marie Ampere: Frederic's Second Father

In a letter to Emmanuel Bailly on 20 May 1847, Frederic Ozanam wrote, "After my poor father who raised me so tenderly, God gave me two persons to take his place at Paris at an age and during a stay filled with dangers: M. Ampere and you. Of the three, only you remain."

Frederic Ozanam's second father was another Lyonnais and a world-class physicist and mathematician and founder of the science of what is now known as electromagnetism. Many say his name daily—ampere—but do not know that the unit of electric current is named after him: Andre-Marie Ampere.

Andre-Marie was a child genius, especially in the field of mathematics. He mastered Latin so he could read the technical textbooks, which at the time were written in that language. Actually, most of Andre-Marie's learning was self-taught with some tutorage from his father.

His father, Jean-Jacques Ampere, and mother, Antoinette de Sutieres Sarcy, lived in the southeast town of Poleymieux-au-Mont-d'Or, twelve miles outside of Lyon. Jean-Jacques was a successful silk merchant and made justice of the peace in 1791. The Ampere home is now a national museum.

Andre-Marie was baptized in the Church of Saint Nizier on 22 January 1775, where his friend Frederic Ozanam was married years later.

In spite of his multiple responsibilities, Jean-Jacques homeschooled Andre-Marie. The youngster never disappointed his teacher. He was a whiz-bang, especially in mathematics and languages.

When Lyon refused to comply with the instructions from Paris, the city was besieged. When it fell, Jean-Jacques was captured, judged as a traitor of the French Republic, and guillotined. Thirteen-year-old Andre-Marie was devastated, and his father's death sent him into a deep depression. He found some consolation in the following years by reflection on his first communion experience, the reading of Antoine-Leonard Thomas's eulogy of Rene Descartes, and the taking of the Bastille in Paris. After his father's death, he had put his studies of mathematics on a hold and only regained his passion for the sciences when he fell in love with Catherine Julie Carron, the daughter of a local blacksmith, whom he first met in April 1796. Although Andre-Marie was madly in love with her, Julie seemed less attracted to him. "He has no manners, is awkward, shy, and presents himself poorly."[61] Still, they married on 2 August 1799 when they were both at the age of twenty-four. Within a year, their son Jean-Jacques was born, named after Andre-Marie's father.

Money was tight. Andre-Marie sought a livelihood by tutoring in the areas of mathematics, chemistry, and languages. In desperation, he took a teaching position thirty miles away, which at that time was a long distance and kept him away from home for extended periods of time.

Andre-Marie was struck with another severe blow when Julie died of tuberculosis on 13 July 1803. Who would help raise Jean-Jacques? Julie's sister stepped forward and took the youngster and raised him. Later, Jean-Jacques would join his father in Paris to attend advanced studies.

Unfortunately, father and son had a difficult relationship. Perhaps the two were too much alike; perhaps they had been separated for too long a time. Both men were temperamental,

---

61 Article: Ampere Biography, J.J. O'Connor and E.F. Robertson, University of St. Andrews, Scotland

subject to periods of depression and outbursts of anger. Andre-Marie's home could not hold the two for extended periods of time. Jean-Jacques found a resolution: He got out of the house as often as possible under the cover of further studies.

Andre-Marie remarried on 1 August 1806. He and his new bride Jeanne-Francoise Potot, whom he called Jenny, had a stormy marriage. They were legally separated in 1808, and Andre-Marie was given custody of their daughter Josephine-Albine who was born on 6 July 1807.

Andre-Marie had his hands full with Albine. She married one of Napoleon's lieutenants in 1827, who turned out to be an alcoholic. In 1830, Albine moved in with her father, and amazingly, her father welcomed her husband into the house. But peace did not last very long. The police had to be called for what we would refer to as domestic violence. The husband left.

Frederic Ozanam met the famous scientist in Lyon at the home of a friend. Andre-Marie learned that Frederic was registering in the School of Law at the Sorbonne and invited his fellow Lyonnais to visit him when he got settled in Paris. Frederic took Andre-Marie up on his invitation shortly arriving in Paris during the first week of November 1831.

Before Frederic knew it, Andre-Marie offered him a room—his son's, Jean-Jacques, who had taken up residence elsewhere. "I offer you table and lodging with me at the same price as your boarding house. You will get to know my son; his library is at your disposal. My sister-in-law, daughter, and son dine with me, and would be good company for you. What do you think?"[62]

Frederic was flabbergasted. He immediately wrote his father for permission and received it. Andre-Marie was a celebrity! It was like a dream come true. Frederic had had a difficult time living in

---

62 Letter, #38, to his father, Dr. Jean-Antoine-Francois Ozanam, 12 November 1831, Paris

the boardinghouse because of the loose talk at the table and the way the other boarders made fun of his adherence to the practices of the faith, such as fasting, abstaining, and attending Mass on Sundays and holy days.

Andre-Marie's scholarship and conversations fed Frederic's brilliant mind, but the new houseguest was also impressed by Andre-Marie's spirituality as well. It was a good match for both the senior gentleman and the youngster and lasted for some eighteen months until Jean-Jacques Ampere returned home to reclaim his room. Frederic had to vacate the premises, but he found a new friend in Jean-Jacques, one that would last until Frederic's death.

Andre-Marie Ampere died in Marseille from pneumonia on 10 June 1836 when he was sixty-one years old. It was a day of great sadness for Frederic. He lost his second father.

The burial took place in Marseille, but the remains were transported to the Montmartre Cemetery in Paris in 1869. Although father and son did not get along well during their lifetime, their remains now lay side by side in Montmartre.

Jean-Jacques Ampere: Friend #1?

The famous Alexis de Tocqueville counted Jean-Jacques Ampere among his friends. The two met for the first time in 1835, and from then on, he became a regular guest at the chateau de Tocqueville, where one of the bedrooms was called the "Ampere room."

Tocqueville describes Jean-Jacques "as a man of spirit ... a man of great heart, pleasant to be with and always trustworthy. His benevolence disposed him to love ... never mean ..." Later, Tocqueville says in a letter about Jean-Jacques, "No one was wittier ... temperament free as a bird's ... character as adaptable enough that he could adopt any life style ... with joy and revel in it."[63]

Who was Frederic Ozanam's closest friend besides his wife, Amelie? That is a hard call, but perhaps it was Jean-Jacques Ampere, a man who in many ways was so different from Frederic. Or was Jean-Jacques more a brother than a friend? He wrote him thirty-three letters that we know about, and in those letters, we can feel their closeness. Frederic knew Jean-Jacques a few years before de Tocqueville. Frederic Ozanam wrote Jean-Jacques: "You promised me the acquaintance of Tocqueville."[64]

Jean-Jacques was the only son of Andre-Marie Ampere, Frederic's second father. While Jean-Jacques and his father were not particularly close, Frederic was close to both father and son.

In an extended tour in northern Europe, Jean-Jacques studied the folk songs and popular poetry of the Scandinavian countries, and in 1830, he presented a series of lectures on Scandinavian and

---

63   Alexis de Tocqueville *Souvenirs;*Tocqueville in a letter to Francisque de Corcelle, 2 October 1854, Portraits: His Friends

64   Letter, #1224, Jean-Jacques Ampere, 13 January 1853, Pisa, Italy

early German poetry in Marseille. The publication of this material was probably the first introduction of the French populace to the Scandinavian and German epics.

In 1831, Frederic moved into Jean-Jacques's room at the Ampere household after he had traveled to Germany to study. Ten years later, he was touring North Africa, Greece, and Italy. Jean-Jacques was a man on the go. His studies, combined with Frederic's, advanced the scholarship of Dante in France. When he was not gallivanting around the world, Jean-Jacques taught at the Sorbonne and became professor of the history of French literature at the College de France. He was honored in 1847 by becoming a member of the prestigious French Academy occupying Seat 37 until his death in 1864.

We see something of the depth of Frederic and Jean-Jacques's friendship in their correspondence. A case in point is Jean-Jacques's trip to Canada and the United States in 1851.

It is quite amazing how much Frederic knew of the United States, and it is probably due to Jean-Jacques's travels more than anything, although we cannot forget that his beloved mother-in-law was born and raised in Norfolk, Virginia. She may have shared some bits of information with her French son-in-law.

The Ozanams were out in the country air in Sceaux with the hope for Frederic's improvement, but his health problems were going from bad to worse. Frederic wrote Jean-Jacques,

> When I so strenuously opposed your transatlantic voyage, I was only actuated by the egoism of friendship. Don't imagine that I am an enemy of the Yankees, and don't, I implore you, get me into any sort of trouble with that great people. They will probably realize the political ideal to which, in my opinion, modern society is tending.

All you tell me about Quebec and Montreal touches me deeply. Above all, the joy you had in finding the name of your illustrious father still living there. I am delighted to see you seated at the family banquet of our brothers ... (Frederic is referring here to members of the Society of Saint Vincent de Paul, which had been established in Quebec in 1846.)[65]

Frederic was happy to hear that Jean-Jacques had been in Boston. He had been there for the Railroad Jubilee, a three-day celebration commemorating the railroad connection between Boston and Canada on September 17–19, 1851. President Millard Fillmore arrived on 17 September and gave a speech, which he later claimed was impromptu. Frederic wrote, "I am far from making small account of the speeches of the President of the United States, and very far from despising those processions of working men of which the calm and well-disciplined democracy of America gives us the spectacle."[66]

He told Jean-Jacques, "You will patronize my wife and help her to set up a flower-stall on Broadway. As for me, I speak English too poorly to exercise my small talents of professor and lawyer, and I see no career open to me but to beat the big drum behind my brother's carriage ..."[67] Frederic was referring to his brother Dr. Charles Ozanam, who incidentally had married a United States citizen.

"Even our little Marie is up to date on your travels. You are teaching her geography, and she knows about America as the country where Mr. Ampere is traveling. May the winds fill your sails in the right direction ... and never carry you ... where our thoughts do not follow you."[68]

---

65 Letter, #1115, Jean-Jacques Ampere, 22 October 1851, Paris

66 Ibid.

67 Ibid.

68 Ibid.

There was one piece of business that Frederic had to do: He had to confront Jean-Jacques on returning to the Catholic Church. Because of their close friendship, Jean-Jacques had shared his innermost feelings with Frederic, but time was running out. Frederic knew his life was coming to an end, and he felt compelled to address the issue.

> You are a Christian by birth, by the blood of your incomparable father. You fulfill all the duties of Christianity toward men, but are there not others to be fulfilled toward God? Must we not serve him and live in close relationship with him? Would you not find this relationship a source of infinite consolation? Would you not find there security for eternity? [69]

How did Jean-Jacques take the letter? He promised that he would pray for fullness of light and did so for fifteen years. He wrote, "I will persevere honestly in seeking for the truth! No one longs for it more sincerely than I do, and every night of my life I send up to God the prayer: Give me light!" God answered Jean-Jacques's prayers. He came back to the church before he died in Pau on 27 March 1864, almost eleven years after his friend Frederic Ozanam.

Tocqueville wrote Jean-Jacques on the second of October 1853 and told him how much he enjoyed his writing about Ozanam and deeply regretted that he had never met the man.

---

69   Letter, #1101, Jean-Jacques Ampere, 24 August 1851, Dieppe, France

Joseph Mathias Noirot: Frederic's Magi

An American newspaper ran an obituary on Wednesday, 27 January 1880 that read, "The Abbé Joseph Mathias Noirot, member of the Academy of Letters at Lyon, France, and an officer of the Legion of Honor, is dead." The Abbé had taught philosophy at the College Royal of Lyon from 1827 to 1852.[70]

Frederic Ozanam speaks of knowing the Abbe as early as May 1830. The priest had been described as an apostle and an apologist. He was Frederic's confidant, mentor, magi, and friend. Frederic completely trusted the man's wisdom, and he on his part may well have known the inner life of Frederic Ozanam better than anyone.

Between fifteen and sixteen, Frederic suffered a crisis of faith, of which he spoke very honestly. And he announced his savior: "It was the teaching of one who was both a priest and philosopher who saved me; he brought light into my mind; I believed henceforth with an assured faith, and touched by this mercy, vowed to consecrate my days to the service of that truth which had given me peace."[71]

How often does God bring good out of bad? Out of his doubts came the dedication of Frederic Ozanam to the service of truth— the driving passion he displayed from that moment of grace to the moment of death.

During Frederic's stay in the Ampere household, he must have shared what he had suffered during his crisis of faith. Andre-Marie Ampere says of his fellow Lyonnais, "All those who studied under this cherished master agree that he had a particular gift of

---

70   New York Times, 27 January 1880, obituaries

71   Disquisitio, op. cit., p.1047

directing and developing each one in his vocation."[72] These were flattering words. Could it be that Ampere knew Noirot more than by reputation?

Ampere says that he used the Socratic method in the classroom; so did Frederic Ozanam in the lecture halls of the Sorbonne. Whenever the abbé saw a young student enrolled in his philosophy class who was full of himself, the professor gently brought him to recognize the fact that he knew very little and "when he had crushed him under the weight of his own weakness, he raised him up"[73] and pointed out to him what he really could do. It sounds much like the cycle of the paschal mystery: life, death, and resurrection. The priest-philosopher took each student through the cycle.

In his biography of Frederic Ozanam, the famous Dominican priest Henri Lacordaire tells us that Noirot saw Frederic as a favorite student. They would take walks together on the outskirts of Lyon as they discussed God and his relationship with humanity. These lively dialogues did much to strengthen Frederic's faith and laid the foundation for his entire life.

The Abbé provides us with an in-depth description of Frederic during this time of his life. He was an elect soul, marvelously endowed by nature in mind and heart, and showed incredible zeal at what he did. He was devoted, modest, cheerful, and joyful, but there was always an undercurrent of seriousness about the young man. He was extremely popular among his peers. He loved a good joke and a fun time. Noirot claims that he never heard of Frederic ever getting into any problem. He was affectionate, sympathetic, and harbored no antipathy or hatred, yet he did react strongly against falsehood and wrongdoing.

This description sounds like a deposition for a person's canonization process. Or perhaps a summary of characteristics

---

72 O'Meara, op. cit., p.9

73 Ibid.

expected in a person older in years and a deep spirituality, but not a young collegian.

Frederic himself later praised his priest-professor for his priesthood and relationship with the students, who, in Frederic's estimation, owed much for the preservation of their faith.

In correspondence with Henri Pessonneaux in 1836 as he was recruiting members for the Society of Saint Vincent de Paul in Lyon, Frederic suggested that he contact the abbé as a possible source for members of the Society, as he would be able to identify good solid candidates.

But the greatest role the priest played in Frederic's life was setting him up to meet his future wife Amelie Soulacroix.

After receiving his bachelor of letters on 2 October 1829, Frederic kept in contact with the abbé until Frederic's death in 1853. The priest continued to teach for twenty-five years afterward and was named to a high administrative position in the French academic divisions, which he held until 1856.

Jean-Baptiste-Henri Lacordaire

When Frederic Ozanam met Lacordaire in 1833, he was a priest of the archdiocese of Paris who had been ordained by Archbishop Hyacinthe de Quelen on 22 September 1827.

In today's parlance, Jean-Baptiste's was a delayed vocation. He had received a degree in law in Dijon, but while in law school had abandoned the faith of his childhood. He relished living in love of liberty and in ignorance of God and the gospel, but Jean-Baptiste was not at peace. He found it in the faith that he had abandoned ten years earlier. Almost immediately after his reconciliation with God and the church, he decided to give his entire life to the service of God.

During the cataclysmic social, political, and religious uprisings during the first half of the nineteenth century, Jean-Baptiste did what other French priests did: look toward the missions in the New World. When John Dubois, SS, bishop of New York, came to Paris recruiting priests for the United States, Lacordaire expressed his desire to volunteer and received permission from his archbishop to leave for New York. But the July 1830 Revolution stopped the process.

In God's providence, Lacordaire met Father Felicite de Lamennais, one of the dynamic lights in the church. Lamennais offered Lacordaire a job as a journalist and coworker in a newspaper, *L'Avenir* ("The Future"). The goal of the paper was its motto, "God and freedom." Lacordaire took the job and forgot about America.

The two priests wrote articles on all aspects of freedom—speech and press—and urged all Catholics to exert their rights. However, the newspaper became too radical, too left of left, and the bishops of France condemned it. Pope Gregory XVI also condemned the writings in *L'Avenir*. Lacordaire conceded, and Lamennais rebelled, eventually leaving the priesthood.

With the press closed to him, Lacordaire turned to lectures, and was he a gifted speaker! In fact, he has been labeled as the greatest preacher of the nineteenth century.

In January 1834, Lacordaire gave a series of talks at College Stanislas in Paris. He was a huge success. Frederic Ozanam sensed that Lacordaire was exactly what the collegians, university professors, and intelligentsia of Paris needed.

Frederic and a few friends sought permission from Archbishop de Quelen to allow Lacordaire to preach a series in Notre Dame Cathedral. The archbishop was not too keen on Lacordaire. After all, his reputation, right or wrong, was more left than right—or center. But the archbishop liked Frederic's idea. He compromised and asked several others to preach. But they were not successful enough in the mind of Frederic Ozanam. He wanted Lacordaire.

Like the man in the gospel, Frederic kept knocking on the door. The archbishop acquiesced. Lacordaire gave the Lenten Conferences of 1835. The rest is history. Some five thousand filled Notre Dame with the archbishop and several other authority figures in the front rows. Part of this was due to some members of the Society of Saint Vincent de Paul who did an amazingly successful job of advertising and promoting the series thanks to Frederic Ozanam's persuasion.

Lacordaire had his own style, which was very different from the ordinary preacher. He addressed issues of the day in light of the church's teachings, and he did it with intelligence and clarity.

After two years, Lacordaire decided that he needed solitude, and during a retreat in Rome, he chose to enter the Dominican Order. He took vows on 12 April 1840 and returned to France. The Dominicans had been reinstated in the country after their suspension during the Revolution. In a short time, Lacordaire was named provincial. His goal: recruit highly qualified men for the order.

Lacordaire pursued Frederic Ozanam. He saw a brilliant mind and outstanding moral character. Although Frederic had two doctorates, law and literature, he was still searching for a definitive vocation. Would it be marriage or priesthood, specifically the Dominicans?

After much prayer and consultation, Frederic made his decision: marriage. He believed that his career was in the university classroom, serving the truth. He wanted to continue visiting the homes of the destitute and bringing them physical and spiritual assistance. His patron and inspiration was first and foremost Saint Vincent de Paul.

Lacordaire and Ozanam remained friends until death. After Frederic's death in 1853, Lacordaire published his biography within three years. Lacordaire deserves a word of great gratitude because he has furnished the world with some unique information about Frederic Ozanam.

Jean-Baptiste Marduel and Claude-Antoine Massucco: Two Spiritual Directors

Msgr. Alphonse Ozanam speaks of Jean-Baptiste Marduel in glowing terms. We learn that the priest was a parochial vicar at the Church of Saint-Nizier in Lyon but left there to assist his cousin of the same name as a cure, or pastor of Saint-Roch, Paris.

As the cure between 1750 and 1770, Jean-Baptiste made vast improvements to the interior of Saint-Roch. He had been successful in soliciting well-known artists of the time to decorate the church. The priest was cure from 1742 to 1848. Unfortunately, the church was located in the center of the French Revolution and was ransacked. Works of art were stolen and destroyed.

Jean-Baptiste was Frederic Ozanam's first spiritual director. Until his death, this saintly priest was also the spiritual director of Alphonse Ozanam. We do not know with certitude if Marduel assisted Alphonse in his decision to abandon his medical career for priesthood or not, but the way Alphonse speaks of him as a director of conscience and his other comments, it would not be inconceivable that he did.

Alphonse tells us that Marduel was his brother Frederic's spiritual father. And Frederic told his friend Francois Lallier that Marduel, "my spiritual father of Paris is here,"[74] was the one who taught him to admire the richness represented in the sacrament of penance.

Father Marduel retired in Paris and lived in a small apartment on the rue Massilor. Until his death, the priest had many spiritual

---

74   Letter, #78, Francois Lallier, 15 October 1834, Lyon

directees. Frederic spoke of Father Marduel's death to his brother Alphonse in a letter of 28 February 1848.

When the Ozanams moved to Italy in 1853 with hope of Frederic regaining his health, he met Father Claude-Antoine Massucco, CM, superior of the Vincentian community in Livorno and rector of the seminary there. Frederic took him as his spiritual director and mentioned Father Massucco in two different letters to his brother Charles and once in correspondence to his brother Father Alphonse. "The superior of the Priests of the Mission who is our strong friend".[75]

Frederic was greatly appreciative of the priest's direction and added this codicil to his last will to express his thankfulness: "Who have overwhelmed me with kindness. God alone can reward" him. [76]

75   Letter, #1311, Charles Benoit, 24 June 1853, San Jacopo pres Livourne, Italy

76   Codicil to Ozanam's Last Will, O'Meara, op. cit., pp. 340-341

Dante: The Many Facets of ...

Dante: poet, theologian, pilgrim, lover ...

During vacation of 1833, Dr. and Mrs. Ozanam and sons made a trip to Italy. Mrs. Marie Ozanam stayed at her sister's home in Florence while the men proceeded to other Italian cities, including Rome. It was quite a vacation. An audience with Pope Gregory XVI and a dinner with Cardinal Joseph Fesch, archbishop of Lyon and uncle of Napoleon Bonaparte, were but two highlights.

How did the young Frenchman, Frederic Ozanam, "become friends" with the great Florentine Dante of the thirteenth century? Frederic provides us with an excellent clue. In his preliminary discourse to *Dante and Catholic Philosophy in the Thirteenth Century*, Frederic Ozanam pinpoints the time and place: the Apostolic Palace in the Vatican when he became taken with Dante while gazing on Raphael's masterpiece *The Disputation of the Sacrament*. Frederic writes,

> In one of the groups composing the assemblage, the specta-
> tor distinguishes a figure remarkable by the originality of
> its character, its head encircled, not by a tiara or miter, but
> by a wreath of laurel. The countenance is noble and aus-
> tere, nowise worthy of such company. A momentary glance
> into the memory brings to mind Dante Alighieri.[77]

The young Ozanam was more than surprised to see Dante in red attire standing in the midst of Pope Julius II, Pope Sixtus IV, and Savonarola. He continues in the preliminary discourse:

---

77   Dante and Catholic Philosophy in the Thirteenth Century, Frederic Ozanam, translated Lucia D. Pychowski, 2nd ed., New York: Cathedral Library Association, 1913, p.47

The question then naturally arises, by what right has the portrait of such a man been introduced among those of the venerated witnesses of the faith, and that by an artist accustomed to the scrupulous observance of liturgical traditions, under the eyes of the popes, in the very citadel of orthodoxy?[78]

Why would Raphael, a master painter, include Dante, a master poet, in such a venerated group of theologians particularly known for their defense of transubstantiation? The question was born then and there at the Vatican palace, and he needed to find an answer. Did the Holy Spirit prompt an insight? Further development certainly occasioned more study, reflection, and in-depth insights.

Friendship was something sacred to Frederic Ozanam. Friends assisted him in keeping the faith, as he had said, of keeping him on the right path to God. Dante's *Divine Comedy* tells how God, through the instrumentality of Beatrice, drew the poet to salvation and, if him, every human being.

It is good to remember that Frederic Ozanam was an excellent linguist. As is seen in the latter days of his life that he spent in Italy, he spoke fluent Italian. He was able to read Dante's masterpiece in its original format. Having been born and raised in his earliest years in Milan, Frederic became well versed in the language, not uncommon for children exposed to another language other than the one spoken at home. Frederic will witness the same phenomenon with his own daughter's proficiency in Italian at her age of eight in 1853 during the family stay at Antignano outside of Livorno.

Frederic mentions Dante for the first time in a letter to his mother several weeks after he is back in school in Paris and then again to her in consequent years before her death. He quotes Dante

---

78   Ibid., op. cit., p.48

to his close friend and First Communion companion, Louis Janmot, in a letter dated 13 November 1836. In a letter to his cousin Ernest Falconnet on 10 January 1837, he wrote, "My interminable thesis on the philosophy of Dante is finished." [79]

Toward the end of 1838, Frederic Ozanam stood at the Sorbonne defending his doctorate of letters. All his preliminary exams had gone well, but the actual defense would be classified as spectacular. Frederic literally wowed the board of examiners.

From his first encounter with Dante in 1833 to that moment in 1838, Frederic had studied the character and genius of the Florentine poet and grew to truly admire the person. At the defense of his doctorate, Frederic revealed Dante as poet and theologian, perhaps what Raphael had seen in Dante and why he had included him among the band of theologians at the bottom right in *The Disputa*. During the questioning by the board of examiners, at Frederic's defense, Dante became alive through Frederic's words and person. Those in attendance were spellbound as they listened to the defender reveal the deceased Italian poet whom he had come to know so intimately through his research and study.

One of the board members, the celebrated Victor Cousin, a renowned philosopher at the Sorbonne and author himself, asked, "Ozanam, how is it possible to be so eloquent?"

Frederic Ozanam received his doctorate. His thesis *Dante and Catholic Philosophy in the Thirteenth Century* was later published and is still available.

It is interesting to see sprinkled throughout Frederic's correspondence, especially to close friends of some education, quotes from Dante's *Divine Comedy*. These quotations appear in the middle of a paragraph to illustrate some point that Frederic was attempting to emphasize.

Dante was a friend until Frederic's death.

---

79   Letter, #139, Ernest Falconnet, 10 January 1837, Lyon

The Magnificent Seven

Seven friends heard a challenge from another student during the course of a discussion, and they had to admit that he was right. They decided to do something for others, namely, the poor after the example of Jesus Christ.

The seven consisted of six college students at the famous Sorbonne in Paris; the day was 23 April 1833. It was a Pentecostal happening as evidenced by the pressing need that was and is met and has continuous internal development and international expansion.

The six collegians, who ranged from ages nineteen to twenty-two, were predominantly students in the school of law except for one in the school of medicine. The seventh person was a thirty-nine-year-old husband and father of six, a Catholic newspaper owner and editor, a promoter of a scholastic discussion group, and proprietor of a pension.

The friends called themselves the Conference of Charity of Saint Vincent de Paul. Their association would evolve shortly into what we know today as the Society of Saint Vincent de Paul. The April date of its foundation fell on the birthday of one of the students, Antoine Frederic Ozanam, who had called for the initial meeting in response to the challenge.

The nonstudent whom the collegians had unanimously requested to be the first president of their fledging operation was Joseph Emmanuel Bailly. The remaining five in the group were Auguste Le Taillandier, Francois Lallier, Jules Devaux, Paul Lamache, and Felix Clave.

The seven were indeed friends. Friendship was an important characteristic—constitutive—for admittance into their organization. In fact, in the beginning, the seven friends seemed to want to exclude any other individuals from their circle. After all these years, now that the Society of Saint Vincent de Paul is truly worldwide, friendship is still an expected characteristic on every level of membership from conference, the basic unit of the organization, to the international lay leadership located in Paris. The expectation is not that friends only invite friends to join them as was evidenced in the origins of the Society, but that members also cultivate friendship once they do join and concentrate on their communal ministry.

Depending on the nationality or culture, members refer to themselves generally as Vincentians after their patron and inspiration Saint Vincent de Paul or specifically as confreres, or brothers and sisters, which are more familial terms.

As Vincentians meet together, pray, and visit two by two the homes of those who are poor or work together in a soup kitchen, food pantry, etc., they interact as friends.

Frederic Ozanam viewed his involvement in the Society of Saint Vincent de Paul as interplay between friends for friends. While some might consider those in need as clients, Frederic was more apt to see them as friends. The members of the Society of Saint Vincent de Paul were friends helping friends. Members of the Society pray at the beginning of every meeting,

> Lord Jesus, deepen our Vincentian spirit of friendship during this meeting, make us responsive to the Christian calling to seek and find the forgotten, the suffering, or the deprived so that we may bring them your love. Help us to be generous with our time, our possessions, and ourselves in this mission of charity.[80]

---

80 Opening Prayers, National Council of the United States, Society of St. Vincent de Paul, Manual, p.72, Saint Louis, Missouri

Joseph-Emmanuel Bailly: Frederic's Second or Third Father?

The Bailly family was deeply devoted to Saint Vincent de Paul. Emmanuel's father, Andre Joseph Bailly, was a close associate of the Vincentian family, which had temporarily entrusted Bailly with a collection of Saint Vincent's manuscripts during the French Revolution. The rebels had little respect for anything sacred, and the Vincentian administration wanted to take no chances with these precious archival materials. Andre Bailly treated them as the true treasures they were. When things in France had calmed down, Bailly returned the letters of the saint back to the Vincentian community.

Andre's brother, Nicholas Bailly, was a Vincentian priest, another reason for endearment to the saint. Nicholas was the last superior of the major seminary at Amiens before the Revolution. Bailly was captured while celebrating Mass, thrown into prison, and died there at the young age of twenty-nine on 16 November 1793.

Emmanuel studied philosophy with the Jesuits at Acheul and theology at the Amiens seminary. He decided to enter the Vincentian novitiate but soon realized that priesthood was not his vocation and left. He saw himself as a person of faith fully engaged in secular society.

In 1819, Emmanuel rented a house in Paris and turned it into a pension. His goal was to provide a safe haven for Catholic students from the French countryside or small cities. Emmanuel wanted to do whatever he could to support their faith while they were obtaining a college education that was anti-Christian and secular. The pension also gave the boarders an opportunity for intellectual stimulus through pertinent and lively discussions. Emmanuel was called "Pere Bailly" as a sign of people's affection.

Emmanuel joined a pious association of laypersons, "The Congregation," which played a conspicuous part in the Catholic revival of 1801 to 1830. Six students started the group in February 1801 under the direction of a former Jesuit, Jean-Baptiste Bourdier-Delpuits. It was at first a new version of something old, very much like one of those sodalities under the invocation of the Blessed Virgin Mary that once had flourished in Jesuit colleges. The police suppressed The Congregation when it was discovered that a few of its members had been disseminating Pope Pius VII's documents, excommunicating Napoleon I (1809).

After the fall of Napoleon, The Congregation was revived under the leadership of Father Pierre Ronsin, SJ, who opened up the group to include both lay members and clerics. Emmanuel's previous association with the Jesuits may explain his knowledge of and relationship with The Congregation, which he joined in 1820.

Although The Congregation per se confined its purpose to religious activities, its members sprouted charitable, social, and educational organizations. Apparently, The Congregation had two branches: Society of Good Studies and Society of Good Works. Emmanuel affiliated himself with the latter group and gave his attention initially to visiting patients in hospitals. The two branches combined in 1828 and operated out of Bailly's building. The liberal press denounced The Congregation as a tool of the Jesuits and for infiltrating governmental administration.

After the Jesuits were ousted from teaching in France in June 1828, The Congregation dropped in popularity and ministry. July 1830 ended its existence, although some of its creations survived, thanks to its members.

Emmanuel Bailly was such a creative person. He never was one to let the topsy-turvy political scene of France beat him or put a damper on what he knew to be a good beneficial concept. He was not afraid to start small. He began an organization named The Conference of History patterned closely after The Congregation's Society of Good Studies, of which he had been its president. This new group would prove providential in its recruitment of outstanding members who played exemplary roles in the renewal of the church.

The Bailly pension filled to capacity. Emmanuel added a second facility, and when these outgrew their locations, in 1825, he bought a larger building at 13 Place de l'Estrapade, which provided ample space for lodging, dining, and meetings.

On 20 July 1830, Emmanuel married Marie-Apolline-Sidonie Vyrayet de Surcy. This was providential also because the July Revolution began days later. Sidonie's father asked that Emmanuel preserve her name, and he did. As a consequence, he himself often has been referred to as Joseph Emmanuel Bailly de Surcy.

The Baillys were proud parents of six children. One daughter, Marie, became superior of the Daughters of Chlotilde and another, Marie-Adrienne, joined the Carmelites but unhappily died in Poland at the early age of twenty-two. The middle son, Bernard, followed his father's trade of journalism and for many years was a contributing editor of *Le Cosmos*, a magazine that reviewed the latest in scientific developments. The oldest and youngest sons, Vincent de Paul and Emmanuel, became Assumptionist priests. Their vocational choice may be due partially to the fact that dynamic, leading Catholics often frequented the Bailly home, one of whom was Emmanuel d'Alzon, founder of the Assumptionists.

Vincent de Paul Bailly was an active member of the Society of Saint Vincent de Paul from his teen years and in 1855 became a member of the Society's Central Council in Paris. He earned his livelihood as a postal worker for years and toward the latter years of his life became the private telegrapher for Napoleon III. After making a retreat in Nimes in 1860, he decided to join the Assumptionists and was ordained to the priesthood in Rome in 1863. The younger brother, Emmanuel, joined him shortly after their father's death in 1861.

Printer's ink must have run in the Bailly bloodstream because in 1883, Vincent de Paul Bailly founded the daily newspaper, *La Croix*, which is still published today in France. He was unfortunately anti-Semitic and contributed to the suppression of his Assumptionist community for several years from France. The priest himself was forced to leave the country and resided in Rome. On the positive side, his vision led to the establishment of La Bonne Presse.

A legitimate question to ask is, in light of their family and father's longstanding affiliation with the Congregation of the Mission, commonly known as the Vincentian priests and brothers, why did not Vincent de Paul and Emmanuel Bailly join them rather than the Assumptionists? Given the facts of their grandparent's love for Saint Vincent de Paul, family members having been Vincentian priests, and their father once a novice in the community, you would surmise that the two Baillys would gravitate toward the Congregation of the Mission. Not so.

There is a positive and negative answer. While he was stationed in Nimes early in his career as telegrapher, Vincent de Paul Bailly had resided with the Assumptionists' founder Emmanuel Alzon. Bailly was greatly influenced by the living spirituality of an excellent priestly role model.

The negative reason for not choosing the Vincentians was their father's inflammatory and legal entanglement particularly with the superior general of the community, Father Jean-Baptiste Nozo, CM. Not only were the legal proceedings extended and convoluted, they were at times nasty. The case involved Emmanuel's brother, Father Ferdinand Bailly, a Vincentian priest, who had ministered at the seminary in Amiens for thirty years. There were questions of accountability and financial appropriateness on the priest's part. Father Bailly won the lawsuit and was awarded a huge amount of money from his own community.

In response, Father Nozo distributed three thousand pamphlets to every diocese of France, magistrates, and various government offices in Paris and in Pas de Calais from where the Baillys originated. Emmanuel swung into action, as the family reputation was at stake, and decided to sue Nozo for defamation of character. Bailly objected most vigorously to the allegation in the circulated pamphlet that he had received money inappropriately from his brother Ferdinand to purchase a house and a business.

Blessed Rosalie Rendu, a Daughter of Charity of Saint Vincent de Paul, sought the intervention of Archbishop of Paris Denis Auguste Affre to settle the dispute by requesting that Bailly drop the suit. Sister Rosalie wanted to assure that any scandal be avoided. But her involvement was not appreciated by the leadership of the Congregation of the Mission. Nozo lost the lawsuit, and Emmanuel Bailly collected a tidy sum with which he purchased property that the newly married Frederic and Amelie Ozanam rented from him. Emmanuel counted on the rental of apartments in this location to provide him with sufficient income for family expenses.

Nozo and his council renewed legal action regarding Father Ferdinand Bailly. After winning two judgments, the priest lost arbitration and was forced to return almost the entire sum that he had previously acquired. The case drew wide attention in the Paris press. Out of charity, the Vincentian leadership agreed to provide Father Bailly with income for the rest of his life. The priest lived in the Parisian suburb of Neuilly, where he died in 1864.

Although Emmanuel Bailly had retired from the top leadership of the Society of Saint Vincent de Paul, he continued his ministry with the Society until the end of his life.

Emmanuel Bailly enlisted in the National Guard in 1848 to help in the defense of Paris and the New Republic against rioters. He joined Frederic Ozanam and Leon Cornudet when they approached Archbishop Affre on 25 June to ask him to quell the revolution to which he agreed.

However, it so happened that the day before, 24 June, General Louis-Eugene Cavaignac was granted full powers, making him, for all practical purposes, France's head of state and dictator. Frederic and Emmanuel accompanied the archbishop to the headquarters of General Cavaignac for permission to attempt the stoppage. With his newfound power, it's a wonder that the general gave his approval, but he did.

Thousands of well-armed and organized rebels were poised behind barricades. Archbishop Affre would not allow Frederic and Emmanuel to accompany him as he scaled a barricade. The hope was that his presence as archbishop would stop the bloody revolution. Unfortunately, he was accidently shot and died the next day.

General Cavaignac forced his way to the Place de la Bastille and crushed the insurrection at the source of operations, its headquarters. The revolution, which had raged from 23 June to the morning of 26 June, was undoubtedly the bloodiest the streets of Paris have ever witnessed, as the general was fairly brutal and showed little mercy toward the rebels.

How much of the legal proceedings between Bailly and the Congregation of the Mission did Frederic know about? If he did know anything, is the presumption correct that the information was coming strictly from Bailly? Or did most of his information come from the press? What impact did the scandal have on Frederic's relationships with a person and an entity he loved dearly?

Emmanuel Bailly died in Paris on 12 April 1861, eight years after Frederic.

Auguste Le Taillandier[81]

The Le Taillandier family moved from their long-established roots in Normandy, France, to Paris so that their son Auguste could pursue studies in the school of law at the Sorbonne. This seems like an extraordinary move on the part of any family, especially of persons who had been merchants in Normandy for years.

Auguste met Frederic Ozanam at the university, and the two became friends. After Frederic moved out of the Ampere residence, he and Auguste shared an apartment together near the parish church of Saint-Etienne-du-Mont. The bachelor Ozanam, almost four years away from his own marriage, shares some thoughts on their sharing of an apartment and on marriage. He wrote Auguste on 21 August 1837,

> Dear friend, two years ago we were living together like brothers, and the memory of that time is sweet. Our two lives were mingled and, after so little an interval ... you are about to have two families, both prosperous, both full of hope.
>
> Fatherhood is at the same time a kind of royalty and a kind of priesthood. Your vocation is difficult but beautiful, serious but certain; you are fortunate to see yourself so near the end of those agitations which torment so great a number of us, anxious and ill-assured of the destiny providence is preparing for us in the world.[82]

---

81   Sometimes Le Taillandier is spelled Letaillandier in Ozanam's letters.

82   Letter, #157, Auguste Le Taillandier, 21 August 1837, Lyon

At this time, Frederic did not know if he wanted to be a Dominican priest or a husband and father.

Le Taillandier and his fiancée Marie Baudry married on 7 August 1838 and parented four children, three daughters and one son.

Auguste had revived many good memories for Frederic. He remembered that Auguste joined Bailly's Conference of History, although he appeared not to be greatly interested in the lively discussions for which the group was known. In 1833, he told Frederic that in his opinion all the talk was precisely that—talk, ineffective and going nowhere. Again in his opinion, he stated that it would be more advantageous to channel that energy and time into some charitable works. According to a mutual friend, Brac de la Perriere, it was Auguste who first thought of having a spiritual meeting for men their age, and he approached both Frederic Ozanam and Francois Lallier with the idea. But according to Paul Lamache in a letter that he wrote some years later to Frederic's brother Alphonse while collecting facts for the biography of Frederic, it was Frederic who first spoke to him about forming a Conference of Charity.

On the night of 23 April 1833, he, Frederic Ozanam, and four other student friends met in the newspaper office of Emmanuel Bailly and held that first historic meeting of the Conference of Charity. They retained their participation in the Conference of History for discussion and academic pursuits, but their Conference of Charity would be for assisting those in need, and in the garrets and on the streets of Paris there were hundreds and hundreds of such persons.

Besides home visitations, which were the hallmark of the Conference of Charity and the soon renamed Society of Saint Vincent de Paul, Auguste devoted much time making visits to prisoners and giving instructions to a group of street kids who were learning the printing trade.

It should be noted that in a letter to Auguste, Frederic refers to him as "the grandfather of all the conferences."[83] It was a high tribute.

In Rouen, Auguste became regional director of one of France's oldest and most distinguished insurance companies. He founded a conference of the Society of Saint Vincent de Paul in Rouen in 1841 and was selected by its membership as their president. His popularity was extremely high; in gratitude to him, the members gave a gift of a stained glass window to Rouen's Saint Godard's Church, which was a portrait of Auguste himself.

Auguste received many honorary titles during his lifetime because of his involvement in Rouen. He particularly was an active member for years on the board of directors of a large city hospital. His final days were devoted to family, friends, his garden, and the conference of the Society of Saint Vincent de Paul. He died in Rouen on 23 March 1886.

83   Letter, #1208, Auguste Letaillandier, 6 December 1852, Bayonne, France

Francois Lallier

Was Francois Lallier Frederic Ozanam's closest male friend? He wrote Francois ninety-four letters! No one else, except his wife Amelie, comes close. Besides, one cannot forget that Francois was godfather for the Ozanam's daughter, Marie.

Francois met Frederic after leaving class one day at the law school. He noticed a small group of students talking, and there in their midst was someone to whom the others were listening. Francois asked himself, "Who is this young rooster to whom those fellows pay so much attention? I recognized Ozanam." [84]Francois joined the group in conversation, and when the others had scattered, "we resumed our conversation."[85] It was the beginning of a friendship that would last a lifetime. Francois and Frederic would talk daily, sometimes having lunch together, near the Church of Saint-Sulpice.

Francois joined Frederic and the Conference of History and became an active participant in its discussions, some of which were quite heated. Francois also volunteered to present a particular topic and its consequent discussion.

On the evening of 23 April 1833, he was one of those at the side of Frederic during the creation of the Conference of Charity. Francois also was one of prime movers along with Frederic in the establishment of the Lenten series when the archbishop of Paris gave his priest Father Jean-Baptiste-Henri Lacordaire permission and he ascended the pulpit at Notre Dame Cathedral on 8 March 1835.

Paul Lamache, one of the original founders of the Conference of Charity, wrote that Ozanam was easily first among friends and Lallier came second. Francois had a strong character, was extremely

84 Baunard, op. cit., p.43
85 Ibid.

kind, possessed sound common sense, showed more reason than imagination, and more solidarity than brilliance. Lamache described Lallier's demeanor as reserved, even cold, but beneath the appearances was a warm heart, melting in close friendship into extreme tenderness. He was serious as a judge combined with a simple and affectionate cordiality. As a consequence, his close friends called him "Pere Lallier."

Francois was renowned for his precise use of French. As president of the Society of the Saint Vincent de Paul, Bailly selected Francois to formulate the main body of the Society's first rule in 1835. He was appointed the Society's secretary-general in 1837. One of his responsibilities was the authoring of the circular letter, which was a major source of communication of the Society wherever it was found. The circular letter proved to be a means of inspiration, motivation, explanation, and information; it also furnished the Society with reports from the basic units of the Society, its conferences.

During Frederic's time in Lyon and his involvement with the Society there, he depended on Francois to promote his vision of the Society within the general headquarters (the Paris Council) and to exert influence on its president, Emmanuel Bailly, who had something of a reputation of being rather laid-back.

In 1839, Francois left Paris, married his sweetheart Henriette Delporte, and returned to his home in Sens where he established a conference of the Society. Frederic visited Francois there after his son Henri was born. When Francois' daughter Lucie died in 1842 only ten months after her birth, Frederic wrote a long letter of consolation to Francois "wet with tears." [86]

Frederic tried to persuade Francois to move first to Lyon and then to Paris. The Lallier's son, Henri, came to study in Paris in 1851 and was often a guest in the Ozanam home. Unfortunately, Henri died at the young age of twenty-four, thirteen years after Frederic's death.

---

86   Letter, #501, Francis Lallier, 9-17 July 1843, Paris

Francois was a well-respected lawyer in Sens, followed by deputy judge in 1852 and then presiding magistrate in 1857. In addition to his ministry with the poor as a member of the Society of Saint Vincent de Paul, Francois maintained an active interest in archeology and in 1844 was a founding member of the Archaeological Society of Sens, a city rich in prehistoric mounds and Roman artifacts. He chaired presidency in the group several times and contributed regularly to its publication. Francois participated in archeological conventions during his lifetime.

Nominated for the National Assembly of the Society of Saint Vincent de Paul in 1848, Francois wrote a paper containing the progressive thought of his friend Frederic Ozanam. Other articles included some of the social justice issues found in the writings of Ozanam, such as single taxing system, abolition of slavery, and universal suffrage. Over the intervening years, Francois published articles on poverty in France and the relationship between poverty and economic systems.

Blessed Pope Pius IX honored Francois with Knight of Saint Gregory the Great and recognized him as a distinguished magistrate, author, and scientist "who carried high and firm the banner of religion." In 1873, Francois also was the recipient of the Cross of the Legion of Honor for years of civil service in Sens.

The international president of the Society of Saint Vincent de Paul, Adolphe Baudon, commissioned Francois to write an account of the Society's origins in anticipation of the Society's golden jubilee. Francois wrote a draft and committed it to the three surviving original founders, Le Taillandier, Lamache, and Devaux. With their collaboration, a brochure was published in 1882, a milestone for the Society.

Francois Lallier died on 23 December 1886 in Sens, France, the city he loved and served so dearly and in which he was so honored.

Paul Lamache

Paul Lamache (1810--1892) was a Normand, born in Saint-Mere-Eglise, a town that played a significant role in the World War II Normandy landings. The United States military forces occupied the town in Operation Boston, one of the first towns to be liberated in the invasion.

Lamache came to Paris to study law at the Sorbonne along with Frederic Ozanam. They were both members of the Conference of History and became close friends. Frederic wrote his mother:

> I have...a circle of friends who discuss daily excellent subjects and that I love as brothers...Lamache, who has the spirit of an artist and almost a knight...what delightful hours we have spent together speaking of country, family, religion, science, literature, legislation, everything beautiful, everything great, everything which ought to be treasured in the heart of man.[87]

Paul Lamache was one of the founding members of the Conference of Charity, whose name was soon changed to the Society of Saint Vincent de Paul. Like the other founders, Lamache was a member of the conference of the parish of Saint-Etienne-du-Mont, Paris, close to the School of Law, Sorbonne. According to Lamache's remarks, this was considered "the mother-conference of all the others."

He wrote extensively on the origin and development of the Society of St. Vincent de Paul: three editions: 1838, 1842, and 1851. As a founder and active participant in the Society, he was

---

87   Letter, #55,to his mother, 19 March 1833, Paris

more than qualified for the task. He collaborated with the *Revue europeanne* and at *l'Universite catholique,* two publications for which Frederic Ozanam also wrote.

Frederic Ozanam speaks about Lamache often in the earlier letters of his life, especially to their mutual friend, Francois Lallier. In one letter, Ozanam praises the excellent article Lamache wrote on Saint Dominic.[88]

Lamache became an attorney-at-law and taught law at Strasbourg and Grenoble and civil code at Bordeaux, France.

On 19 March 1844, Paul Lamache married Henriette Lebon d'Humberin. They parented two sons. During the siege of the Franco-Prussian war, the two Lamache sons who were in the military were captured and held as prisoners of war. Strasbourg was ceded to Prussia in the Frankfort Treaty of 1871.

Paul Lamache was quite active in the conference of the Society of St. Vincent de Paul in Strasbourg. He was president of the conference for a number of years. The members of the Society had a good working relationship with the city government and mutually cooperated for the common good of those in need.

Lamache never retired from his active ministry as a member of the Society. Members were greatly edified by the old man of over eighty years who still climbed the stairs to the attics where the poor lived. He was sometimes accompanied by one of his grandchildren.

One of his shining virtues was that of humility. He never promoted himself as one of the founding fathers of the Society of St. Vincent de Paul.

---

88   Letter, #682, Francois Lallier, 1 June 1846, Paris

Felix Clave

Felix (1811-1853) is the most mysterious of the seven founders of the Society of St. Vincent de Paul. Although Frederic Ozanam suffered physically from various ailments, Felix Clave certainly suffered character assassination as well as the loss of his reputation stemming from the Madame Lafarge fiasco. Because of his entanglement with Lafarge, his photo has been excluded from the portraits of the seven founding fathers of the Society of St. Vincent de Paul.

Clave had been a follower of Saint-Simonianism: men with dreams of replacing Christianity with a utopian-socialist doctrine.[89] He abandoned his allegiance to the movement seemingly through the example and explanations that he heard from Ozanam and other Catholics at the meetings of the Conference of History.

There is no doubt that Clave was one of the pioneers of the Conference of Charity; he was present in the offices of Emmanuel Bailly during the inaugural meeting.

Clave is listed on the 1834 roster of the Society at the parish of Saint-Etienne-du-Mont along with many other significant names.[90] He was one of the initial members of the conference at the parish church of Saint-Phillippe-du-Role.[91] This, as well as the conference located at the Church of Notre-Dame-de-Bonne-Nouvelle, was the first new conferences added by the Society after its foundation in 1833.

Clave left Paris in 1838 and landed in Algiers. And it appears

---

89 A system of socialism rather than religion per se in which the state owns all the property and the worker is entitled to share according to the quality and amount of his/her output.

90 Disquisitio, op. cit, p.353-354.

91 Disquisitio, op. cit., p.219, note 86

that he was bent on starting a conference of the Society there with endorsement of the bishop. Frederic Ozanam wrote:

> At Algiers, under the auspices of its saintly Bishop Dupuch, an association is formed where Clave and many of our old friends form the nucleus.[92]

Prior to the beginning of the Society in Algiers, Bishop Dupuch had attended a meeting of the conference at Saint-Suplice in Paris and had given the young members a short presentation.[93] Obviously, he liked what he saw and heard and was open to Clave and others starting up a conference of the Society of St. Vincent de Paul in his diocese.

As in most of our lives, there was another side to Clave.

After Mass one Sunday, Clave met Marie de Nicolai, a woman of a higher social class than he. Their attraction ended abruptly when Marie discovered that Clave was the son of a mere schoolteacher and possessed little wealth or social status. Marie's close friend, Marie Capelle (later known as Marie Lafarge) entered the mix.

Capelle learned much about Felix Clave: he was a Spaniard and author. He was definitely of a lower class without wealth or prestige, yet Capelle loved him. It became a triangular relationship, more convoluted than not.

Clave left France for Algiers; he saw this was going nowhere.

Capelle married a man whom she never loved thinking he had money and status. The truth was that one of her uncles set it all up including the services of a marriage broker.

---

92 Disquisitio, op. cit., p255. Antoine-Adolphe Dupuch (1800—1856) was named the first bishop of Algiers in 1838; he resigned in 1846. His principal consecrator was Ferdinand-Auguste-Francois Donnet, Cardinal Archbishop of Bordeaux, France, who, as a parish priest, had given the First Communion retreat to Frederic Ozanam and made such a lasting impression on him.

93 Disquisitio, op. cit., p.430

The man was Charles Pouch-Lafarge, the date of the marriage was 10 August 1839. The new bride, Marie Lafarge, found everything wrong and disgusting. She wrote friends that everything was heavenly. Marie began her move: get rid of her husband with arsenic.

As arsenic has many similar effects as cholera, Marie thought that she could get away with her scheme. Besides, arsenic was then often used to kill rats, and there were plenty of them around the residence.

A young woman, Anna Brun, became suspicious. She saw Marie putting a white power in the food and drink of her sick husband.

After a series of improvable investigations of Marie's use of arsenic, the authorities finally apprehended and arrested her. In the meantime, it was uncovered that Marie had stolen jewels from her friend, Nicolai. Of course, Marie denied such a dastardly deed, but the diamonds were found in Marie's room.

Marie invented a story and brought Felix Clave into the ring. She said that Clave had threatened to reveal his romance with Nicolai unless he was paid off. Again, nothing but lies.

Her murder trial became headline news: one of the first trials to be followed by the public through the media of daily newspapers, and because she was the first person to be convicted largely on forensic toxicological evidence.

Marie Lafarge was found guilty of theft and murder, but during the entire time she was in prison, she continued to implicate Clave and, in the process, further ruin his character and reputation.

Clave resettled in France and married, yet his physical and mental health were deeply damaged. He authored several books, among them collections of poetry and a book on Blessed Pius IX, to whom Frederic Ozanam and his wife had spoken in Rome while he was on a sabbatical for health reasons. Ozanam greatly admired the pontiff.[94]

---

94   Letter, #717, Alphonse Ozanam, 17 February 1847, Rome.

Clave died at forty-two years of age, the same year as Ozanam: 1853.

One wonders if Charles Dickens did not have Madame Lafarge in mind when he wrote "A Tale of Two Cities." The novel is set in London and Paris before and after the French Revolution and was published in 1859.

Significant characters in the book were "Defarges." Madame Defarge was vicious and vengeful, a revolutionary. From what is known, Dickens often drew from groups of the time for names of his characters. It may well be that the names of "Monsieur and Madam Defarge" were deliberately chosen.

Madame Defarge and Madame Lafarge were a match.

Jules Devaux

Like his friends Paul Lamache and Auguste Le Taillandier, Jules Devaux hailed from the Normandy region of France. He was born on 18 July 1811 in the town of Colombieres, Calvados.

After attending the College Royal of Caen, Jules came to Paris to follow in the footsteps of his father, a medical doctor. There at the Sorbonne he met Frederic Ozanam for the first time, although Jules was in the school of medicine, not law as Frederic. They actually met while participating in the Saturday Conference of History sessions. Perhaps because he was in the field of medicine and not law, Jules seemed to have taken a more passive stance with the study-discussion group.

Jules Devaux was one of the original seven founders of the Society of Saint Vincent de Paul. From what is conjectured, it was he who walked around the room at that first meeting in April 1833 with his hat held behind his back and took up a collection for the poor and needy. Jules was chosen as the first treasurer of the Conference of Charity and later the first treasurer of the general council, the top administrative unit of the Society.

There is some evidence that Jules may have worked with Blessed Rosalie Rendu in the Mouffetard district of Paris at that time. Regardless, it was he who Emmanuel Bailly requested contact Sister Rosalie, the Daughter of Charity of Saint Vincent de Paul, to mentor the newly formed Conference of Charity.[95] This Jules did, and Sister Rosalie immediately approved their intentions and took them under her wing. It cannot be forgotten that Sister Rosalie Rendu was the Blessed Mother Teresa of her

---

95 Baunard, op.cit., p.71-72

day in Paris. Her reputation was huge and flawless. Her "salon" was where the highest politicians and church hierarchy to the poorest of the poor came for counsel and assistance. Whoever came waited their turn. When the French government gave her a medal of recognition for her public service, which she at first did not want to accept, Napoleon III even came to her.

Sister Rosalie taught the members of the Conference of Charity the nuts and bolts of ministering to God's poor and how to use *bons*, the vouchers for bread and coal.

Henri-Dominique Lacordaire wrote:

It was she (Sister Rosalie), who, from the beginning oriented the Conference of the Society.[96]

Mr. Leveque, a friend of Emmanuel Bailly, first president of the Society of St. Vincent de Paul, and a top administrator of the Bureau of Public Assistance, wrote:

As administrator of the Bureau of Charity for the XIIth arrondissement I had from 450 to 500 indigent households, for whom Sister Rosalie was…the visible hand of Providence. I asked Sister Rosalie to make a choice and put the conference in contact with those she considered better disposed to welcome the visits of our novices in this practice of charity.[97]

Jules left Paris in 1839 after completing his degree in medicine and settled in Trivieres, Normandy. After his mother's death, he suspended his medical practice and traveled in Europe, particularly in Germany. Out of his love for the Society of Saint Vincent de Paul, he attempted to establish a conference there but did not succeed.

On 10 April 1848, Jules married Louise Alice Pasquet in

---

96   Sister Rosalie Rendu: A Daughter of Charity on Fire with Love for the Poor, Sister Louise Sullivan, D.C., Vincentian Studies Institute, Chicago, 2006, p.209; see footnote 457.

97   Ibid., op. cit. p.210. Cited also by Marcel Vincent in *Ozanam, une jeunesse romantique* (Paris, 1994), 275-276.

Paris, and they had one son, who strove to keep his father's memories alive by writing a book.

The remaining days of his life have gone unrecorded. Jules died in Paris on 27 October 1880.

Leonce-Dominique Curnier

Look at the database of French MPs and you will find the name of Leonce-Dominique Curnier, a member of the Legislative Body of 1852–1857.

Leonce was born and raised in Nimes, France, on 22 November 1813 and died in Paris on 29 June 1894. His family was involved in the silk industry of Nimes, not the famous fabric for which the city was renowned and from which we have derived the word *denim* used in blue jeans.

Leonce came to Paris to complete his art studies in Lyon. He remembered when Frederic Ozanam and he interacted for the first time. It was at the end of 1830 in a classroom at the College Royal of Lyon. There was a large number in the particular art class, and the conversations had been taxing most moral values. The eighteen-year-old Frederic Ozanam, who up to that point always appeared quite gentle and calm, stood up. He had had it! Frederic grew animated, became indignant, and then demanded silence. "In a firm but restrained tone he proclaimed his Catholic faith, without, at the same time, saying one word that could hurt the feelings of those misguided young men." [98] Sitting back down, Frederic shook Leonce's hand, a gesture of friendship that lasted for life.

In his biography of Ozanam, Leonce reminisced about their frequent walks together along the banks of the Saone River in Lyon. Frederic shared his devotion to the Blessed Virgin Mary; her shrine of Notre Dame de Fourviere overlooking the city of Lyon was especially dear to him. Leonce attributes his friendship with

---

98   La Jeunesse de Frederic Ozanam, Dominique-Leonce Curnier, 3rd edition, chapter II

Frederic Ozanam as a gift of God's mercy. Frederic's relationship and sharing of his own faith helped to keep Leonce on the straight and narrow. Leonce says that Frederic's example preserved many of their peers in the faith. "I am perhaps the first who was thus saved from ruin."[99]

Frederic and Leonce kept their friendship alive through correspondence. Frederic wrote ten letters to Leonce, and he wrote nine to Frederic. Their personal involvement in the Society of Saint Vincent de Paul also brought them together occasionally. Leonce founded the first conference of the Society of Saint Vincent de Paul outside of the Parisian environs at Nimes in 1837. At the end of October 1834, Frederic wrote a letter to Bailly, the head of the Society, "[Leonce] is the son of one of the better-known businessmen of Nimes, and he is a businessman himself and is constant with the working class of that city."[100]

Leonce became active in local and regional government. In 1852, the year before Frederic's death, Leonce stood as a Legitimist (political) with the approval of the bishop of Nimes, Jean-Francois Cart, and Leonce's uncle, Marie-Dominique-Auguste Sibour, Archbishop of Paris. Unfortunately, Leonce would learn of his uncle's murder five years later; a priest stabbed him to death. Leonce held the position of Receiver General of Finance in the Gard, in the Lower Rhine, and in the Pas-de-Calais. He retired as paymaster general on 8 May 1879, fifteen years before his death.

Leonce authored several books, especially a two-volume work on *The Life of Cardinal de Retz and His Time*, which was quite insightful. For members of the Society of Saint Vincent de Paul, his book *La Jeunesse de Frederic Ozanam* was the one

---

99 Ibid.

100 Letter, #79, Emmanuel Bailly, end of October 1834, Lyon

they appreciated the most. In this biography of 1888, Leonce wrote that he believed he saw Frederic in heaven, sitting between Saint Vincent de Paul and Saint Francis de Sales. Whatever the reality, it certainly says much of what he thought of his friend in life and in death over the years—an excellent position to have.

Alexandre-Marie-Leon Cornudet

With his health failing, death imminent, and his close friend François Lailler living in Sens, France, Frederic Ozanam wanted someone nearby and trustworthy to keep an eye on his young daughter Marie. The person he chose was Leon Cornudet. Although François was Marie's godfather, Leon was considered her protector. As it turned out, Leon was an excellent choice, as he outlived Frederic by twenty-three years. His obligation ceased when Marie married Laurent Laporte in 1866.

Although Leon Cornudet was five years older than Frederic, they were friends from college days at the Sorbonne. During this time, both men became active members in the Society of Saint Vincent de Paul. Although Leon was not one of the founders of the organization, he was certainly a member from its earliest days. Later in his life, Leon's son and son-in-law also played roles in the Society.

Frederic mentioned to Theophile Foisset that Leon Cornudet was "one of my best friends"[101]and told his brother Charles that Leon was one of his particular friendships.[102] Frederic and Leon kept in touch by correspondence until a few months before Frederic's death.

Leon came from a line of wine merchants and government positions. At first, he was associated with Martin du Nord, procurator general of the royal court at Paris and his bureau chief in the Ministry of Public Works. The remainder of his political career was in the council of state as auditor, master of requests, councilor, and section president until the council's suppression in

---

101 Letter, #1111, Theophile Foisset, 25 September 1851, Sceaux

102 Letter, #1195, Charles Ozanam, 14 November 1852, Bayonne

1870. Because of Leon's prestige and expertise in legal matters, he played a significant role in the furtherance of the Society of Saint Vincent de Paul.

In 1844, both he and Frederic became joint vice-presidents of the Council General of the Society and were responsible for the election of a new president general to replace the retiring Emmanuel Bailly. In a letter to Bailly, Frederic recommended Leon Cornudet as candidate for presidency, but Bailly did not support the idea.

Frederic mentions in his letters to his fiancée having dinner with the Cornudets. Leon married his sweetheart Marie-Eudoxie Chappotin de Saint-Laurent on 15 May 1839. After Frederic's death, Amelie and her daughter Marie often ate dinner with Leon and Eudoxie.

The Cornudets had five children. They named their son born in 1848 after Frederic Ozanam, Louis Marie Frederic Cornudet. Their daughter Elisabeth played an important role in the canonization process of Frederic Ozanam. When the ecclesiastical tribunal met to examine witnesses who could testify to the life, virtues, and reputation for holiness of Ozanam, among the thirty-one witnesses called to give testimony, Elisabeth Cornudet was the only eye witness who had personally known Frederic, his wife Amelie, and their daughter Marie. In fact, Elisabeth was chosen as Marie's tutor after Frederic's death in 1853. Elisabeth passed away on 2 June 1927.

Leon Cornudet died on 8 March 1876; Eudoxie outlived him by eighteen years.

Priests

Frederic Ozanam had a good number of priest friends, as priests held a special place in his heart. After all, his oldest brother Alphonse was a priest.

Then there was Abbé Mathias Noirot, his mentor and former philosophy professor, who helped him ride through a crisis of faith in his middle teen years.

Father Jean-Baptist Marduel was Frederic's long-standing spiritual director who knew his interior life better than anyone. Marduel was a part of Frederic's life until the priest's death in 1848.

Father Jean-Baptist Lacordaire, first a diocesan priest and then a Dominican, first met Frederic in 1831 and became a close friend.

Out of the four priests mentioned, two of them wrote biographies of Frederic Ozanam. This fact alone says much of the enduring friendships.

One can't forget the deep impression that the words of Father Francois-Auguste Donnet made on Frederic during the First Communion retreat when the youngster was thirteen.

Frederic was acquainted with many other priests. Most of the relationships went well, and a few did not, one example being Father Robert de Lamennais, who went off the deep end doctrinally and ended up leaving the priesthood.

One thing stands out: Frederic did not hesitate to voice his opinion to priests concerning social justice issues. Often his comments were directed to his priest brother Alphonse.

Frederic Ozanam was a champion of the working class. He spent time on Sundays talking to workers in the crypt of the

Church of Saint-Sulpice. He visited the homes of the poor in the cities of Paris, Lyon, and even during vacation time in London. He had a good handle on the problems of the common worker. He told his priest brother Alphonse,

> If a greater number of Christians, and, above all, of priests had but occupied themselves with the working class these last ten years, we should be more secure of the future; all our hopes rest on the little that had been done in this direction up to the present.

> I am going to have a meeting of professors at my house this afternoon, where we shall discuss the feasibility of establishing public classes and a sort of a night school for these good fellows. The Carmelite priests will give us what help they can, and the archbishop gives us the location.[103]

Frederic cautioned his brother about his new assignment at Lille, France:

> Occupy yourself with the domestics as with masters, with workers as with the rich. This is from now on the only way of salvation for the Church of France. It must be that the pastors renounce their small bourgeoisie parishes, elite flocks in the midst of an enormous population which do not know them. It must be that they occupy themselves not only with the indigent, but, above all, with this class of poor who do not ask for alms, but who are yet attracted by special preaching, by associations of charity, by affection shown them, and which touches them more that one believes. It is now more than ever one ought to

103 Letter, #789, Alphonse Ozanam, 15 March 1848, Paris

meditate on a beautiful passage in the Letter of Saint James, chapter 2:1–9.[104]

After the February Revolution of 1848, three extraordinary persons, two priests and one layman—Father Henri Lacordaire, Father Henri Maret, and Frederic Ozanam—founded a newspaper called *l'Ere Nouvelle* (The New Era). The paper defended the teachings of Pope Pius IX (now Blessed Pius IX), who had plenty of critics.

Frederic wrote twenty-eight articles for the newspaper. In one, he wrote,

> Priests of France do not be offended at the freedom of speech that a layman uses in appealing to your zeal as citizens! The time has come for you to occupy yourselves with those other poor who do not beg, who live by their labor, and to whom the right of labor and the right of assistance will never be secured in such a way as to guarantee them from the want of help, of advice, and of consolation.
>
> The time has come when you must go and seek those who do not send for you, who hide away in the most disreputable neighborhoods, have perhaps never known the church or the priest, or even the sweet name of Christ.
>
> Do not ask how they will receive you, but rather those who have visited them, who have ventured to speak to them of God, and who have not found them more insensible to a kind word and a kind action than the rest of humankind.
>
> If you fear your inexperience, your timidity, the insufficiency of your resources, unite in associations. Take advantage

104 Letter, #802, Alphonse Ozanam, 12 and 21 April 1848, Paris

of the new laws to form yourselves into charitable confraternities of priests. Use all the influence you have with Christian families and urge them to give; press them in season and out of season, and believe that in urging them voluntarily to give of themselves, you are sparing them the unpleasant process of being despoiled by ruder hands.

Do not be frightened when the wicked rich, irritated by your pleading, treat you as communists. They treated Saint Bernard as a fanatic and fool. Remember your fathers, the French priests of the eleventh and twelfth centuries, saved Europe by the crusades; save her once more by the crusade of charity, and, as it involves no bloodshed, be you its first soldiers.[105]

As a person who actually visited the working class and the destitute in their homes through his membership in the Society of Saint Vincent de Paul, Frederic spoke from experiential knowledge, not from some theoretical theory.

---

105 Disquisito, op. cit., p.928, gg, Extracts from *l'Ere Nouvelle*, Number 10, 11 January 1849 (Melanges 1, pp.264-269)

Women in Frederic Ozanam's Life

A quick cursory read of Frederic Ozanam's life may give the impression that there were few women in his life. His list of friends appears to be all of the masculine gender. Biographers and authors emphasize the major players in his academic world and apostolic life, all who were indeed male. This has much to do with the French mentality and customs of the nineteenth century, especially in both fields of endeavor, academics and apostolates. But a closer look and a deeper read of Frederic Ozanam's biography reveals another story. Women held significant roles in his life, and he cherished those relationships and friendships.

We start chronologically with Frederic's mother Marie. She was his primary teacher at the early age of homeschooling, and his sister Eliza, of whom he wrote so passionately after her sudden death at nineteen, was his first instructor. Then there was Guigui, the housekeeper and more, whom he knew and loved from birth to death and who was a part of his flesh and blood.

The girl of Frederic's dreams was Amelie. It was love at first sight, a love relationship of which all stand in awe but few rarely duplicate a love affair that lasted to his deathbed.

Their daughter Marie was the fruit of their love. If anything on earth could have tempted Frederic to not die at such an early age, it would have been her and his desire to educate her personally as his mother and sister did him.

Outside of the inner blood circle, there was a remarkable woman, Sister Rosalie Rendu, D.C., the Daughter of Charity of Saint Vincent de Paul. She was another French person who hailed from a different part of their beloved country but who, like Frederic, has been declared among the blessed of the Catholic church.

While we must credit Frederic's mother and father in planting the seeds of love of the poor by their extraordinary example, we must acknowledge Sister Rosalie for educating him and the other original members of the Society of Saint Vincent de Paul in the nitty-gritty of how best to minister to the poor, especially in the Mouffetard area of Paris, the poor who had been categorized by French academicians as dangerous individuals. Sister Rosalie furnished the members of the new organization of charity with the nuts and bolts of visiting the poor in their homes, especially so many lost in the garrets of the tenements, and with vouchers for bread and coal.

Besides Sister Rosalie's practical instruction on ministry to God's poor, she helped to inculcate into Frederic and the other men a deeper love and appreciation for her patron Saint Vincent de Paul. Rosalie helped turn them into Vincentians—disciples of Saint Vincent de Paul.

We cannot omit reference to Frederic's relationship with the other Daughters of Charity in Sister Rosalie's community. It would be inexcusable to exclude them from consideration because these Daughters of Charity worked in close collaboration with the members of the Society of Saint Vincent de Paul—Vincentians— as the group grew and matured over the years.

There are hundreds of jokes about mothers-in-law and their relationship—or lack of relationship—with their sons-in-law and vice versa, but the relationship between Frederic Ozanam and Zelie Soulacroix was extraordinary. She was his mother, and that was what he called her. Zelie replaced his earthly mother after his biological mother's death. Frederic wrote her and his father-in-law 176 letters. He loved her presence; she met the ship at the port of Marseille when the dying Frederic arrived from Livorno, Italy. Zelie was with him when he entered eternal life.

While Frederic dealt only with men in the lecture hall of the

Sorbonne, he ministered to numerous women in the ghetto of Mouffetard and elsewhere, including London while on vacation. His first celebrated case as a member of the Society of Saint Vincent de Paul was that of a physically abused woman and children by the man with whom she was living without the benefit of marriage. Frederic successfully and quickly got her out of Paris and back home to safety. How many other such cases there were, we don't know.

Were there many women in Frederic Ozanam's life? Oh yes. Many.

Frederic Ozanam:
A Dreamer Who Dreamed Big

When we are dreaming alone, it is only a dream. When we are dreaming with others, it is the beginning of reality.

—Dom Helder Camara[106]

Dreams usually have a history: long-range reflection, thinking, planning, organizing, and collaboration. Dreams take hard work, endurance, patience—and sometimes several attempts after several failures.

Frederic Ozanam had dreams, king-sized dreams—the beginnings of realities. He had three major dreams, which I classify as academic, apostolic, and vocational.

He titled his academic dream *The Demonstration of the Catholic Religion from Historical Religions and Moral Beliefs in Antiquity*. He realized that it could take him a lifetime of scholarship and authorship. He never completed his academic dream although he put quite a dent into it by his publications of various books. Death stopped the dream, not ennui, frustration, or over-involvement. Weeks away from the end of his life, Frederic said, "If anything consoles me, in leaving this world without having accomplished what I wished to do, it is that I have never worked for the praise of men, but always for the service of the truth." [107]

Frederic's apostolic dream was first "a vast and generous association for the assistance of the working classes in France,"[108]

---

106 Dom Helder Camara, Archbishop of Recife, Brazil, lived 1909 to 1999. He was a champion of the poor and an exemplar of humility.

107 O'Meara, op. cit., p.343

108 Letter, #77, Ernest Falconnet, 21 July 1834, Paris

but he expanded that dream, which was to embrace the world in a network of charity. His death did not stop this dream because the Society of Saint Vincent de Paul, of which he was a principal founder, is fulfilling that dream by its worldwide presence and ministry in more than 145 countries around the world.

It cannot be overlooked that Frederic Ozanam was one of the first precursors of social justice in the church. As the Society continues to address systemic change at the root causes of poverty in the world by the practice of the virtues of justice and charity, Frederic's dream continues to become a reality. "Think locally, act globally" is being fulfilled by those men and women of the Society of Saint Vincent de Paul.

His third major dream was his personal vocation in life. He had a solid career; in fact, he was the recipient of two doctorates: law and literature. His vocational dream was realized when he married the girl of his dreams, Amelie Josephine Soulacroix, and they became the proud and thankful parents of a daughter, Marie.

In some respects, Frederic had another dream, which, although was not specified, was actualized. This was a network of friendship. Frederic, by personal encounters and prolific correspondence, maintained and broadened a network of friends among family, peers, colleagues, students, acquaintances, and officials of various agencies. The impression is that once Frederic Ozanam met a person, he or she was one of his friends and vice versa. Frederic's moral integrity, holiness, and etiquette attracted others.

Frederic's Friends

In High Places

The Many Names of God

Among the multiple gifts of Frederic Ozanam, one was his ability to write poetry and of a high caliber. This is evident from his childhood; there are a number of his early poems available due to the foresight of one of his secondary teachers at the College Royal of Lyon, Mr. Urbain Legeay.

During his adulthood, Frederic frequently composed poems for special occasions, especially for his wife Amelie. Before he died, he left a poem to be presented to her after he had passed. The verses express his deep abiding love for her.

Frederic's poetic skill surfaced in his regular writings. Perhaps this skill was due partly to his extensive traveling throughout Europe where he had seen so many beautiful landscapes and scenes of nature. Perhaps it was due partly to his love for sacred Scripture, especially the psalms; Frederic spent hours reflecting on them and his capability to read them in their original language certainly would have benefited his creative writing. Perhaps it was due partly to the high sensitivity of his makeup; he never shied away from expressing his emotions.

In a poetic-type prose written from Biarritz, France, to his friend Alexandre Dufieux, Frederic speaks of God in creative language uncommon to most people,

> In other trips, my mind was distracted by the works of man. In this land, where man has done little, I see only the works of God, and I now say, with all the ardor of my faith, God is not only the great Geometer, the great Legislator, he is also the great Artist. God is the Author of all poetry, he has spilled it in waves within creation,

and if he wished the world be good, he also wished it beautiful.

Quite differently, tell me why these beautiful summits of the Pyrenees convey with so much expansion their peaks of pink granite to heaven? Why they slip out from their sides such leaping cascades, such boisterous torrents, and so pure?

Yes ... by the brink of those cascades where none but the chamois comes to quench his thirst, in the midst of those wilderness where the flowers open their cups only to perfume the solitude of the Most High.

David visited the heights of Lebanon when he cried out, *Mirabilis in altis Dominus!* (Marvelous is the Lord in the heights!) He had contemplated the ocean when he said *Mirabiles eltationes maris!* (Marvelous are the uprisings of the sea!)[109]

Frederic gave God names so differently from many: the great Geometer, Legislator, supreme Artist, and Author of all poetry.

Frederic continues his description of the landscape:

We, too, have stood here by the seashore, and we are never wearied of the grand spectacle it displays to us daily. Everyone knows that the ocean has infinite majesty, but it is only in approaching it that we learn how she is full of grace.

---

109 Letter, # 1193, Alexander Dufieux, 6 November 1852, Biarritz. The translation of the Latin phrases is by the author.

We just returned, my wife and I, all enchanted from the setting of the sun. The star was about to disappear behind the mountains of Spain, whose bold outlines we can see from here standing out against a perfectly beautiful day.

The mountains dipped their feet into a luminous and golden mist that floats above the sea. The rays followed one another, green, azure, sometimes tinted with rose and lilac; then they come to die on the beach of sand, or else break against the rocks that are white with foam. The wave, coming from afar, rises against the cliffs and danced over them in sheaves of spray with all the elegance of those waters that art plays in the garden of kings.

But, here, in the domain of God, the games are eternal. Each day they recommence and vary each day according to the power of the winds and the height of the waves.[110]

Here is the domain of God where the games are eternal.

---

110 Ibid.

Jesus: Master of Disguises

Jesus has many faces; he is the master of disguises. Frederic Ozanam was familiar with Jesus' disguises. He knew his friend when he saw or heard him.

The Vatican II Constitution on the Sacred Liturgy speaks about the presence of Jesus. He is present in the sacrifice of the Mass both in the person of his minister and by his power in the sacraments so that when a priest or deacon baptizes, it is really Christ himself who baptizes. Christ is present in his Word since it is himself who speaks when the Holy Scriptures are read in church. Lastly, he is present, "For where two or three are gathered in my name, I am there among them" (Matthew 18:20).

One's First Communion—the day when a person receives for the first time the body and blood, soul and divinity of Christ—is the day that a good number of people always remember: one's first suit or white dress and new shoes; a new, shiny-covered prayer book and first brown scapular; a brand-new rosary; the excitement of the class; the group photo; the presence of the grandparents, godparents, and other family members; the cards and gifts; and the meal and party at the house afterward. Memories.

For Frederic Ozanam, First Communion was a day that he kept in his heart. He referred to it from time to time in his correspondence, as he saw his First Communion as a significant point in his life.

Prior to the day, there was a retreat for the young teenagers preached by Father Francois-Auguste-Ferdinand Donnet, who had been ordained on 7 March 1819. Father Donnet held three positions: professor, parochial vicar, and home-mission preacher in Lyon and Tours.

Frederic took notes during Father Ferdinand-Auguste-Francois Donnet's[111] conferences, which he saved; obviously, they meant something to him. Although the priest's main Lenten theme was conversion, one of the points that he emphasized was that it was in their training as young men at College Royal of Lyon to be good Christians and good citizens of France. "Young men, it is in your training here to be good Christians...at the same time to be good citizens and to learn to fill with honor the careers in which you would be called upon to serve your God and your country."[112] In all honesty, it sounded like something that Frederic could have heard from his father the doctor and ex-military officer and perhaps did! Whatever, Frederic Ozanam never forgot those words of Father Donnet.

First Communion took place on Thursday before the Feast of Pentecost in the Church of Saint-Pierre des Terreaux in Lyon, close to the Ozanam home. The date was 11 May 1826; Frederic was thirteen years old. Later, Frederic wrote, "O day of happiness! May my tongue cleave to my palate if I forget thee! I have changed well, I have become modest, gentle, and unfortunately I have become a little scrupulous. I perhaps have become more industrious and remained always quiet proud and impatient."[113] Years later, he wrote Charles Hommais, who was one of the founders of the Society of Saint Vincent de Paul in Rouen that "[it is] Christ who is in the inexpressible sweetness of communion ..."[114] In a letter to his mother, Frederic narrated an adventure that he and several collegians undertook for the celebration of Corpus Christi when Frederic was twenty years old. It was something that young, devout

---

111 Father Donnet was consecrated Coadjutor Bishop of Nancy and within two years Archbishop of Bordeaux, France, and a Cardinal in March 1862.

112 Baunard, op. cit., p.8

113 Letter, #12, Auguste Materne, 5 June 1830, Lyon

114 Letter, #1143, Charles Hommais, 16 June 1852, Paris

college students might do: daring, courageous, and harebrained (Frederic used this term himself).

At 10:30 in the morning, they participated in a Corpus Christi procession at Nanterre, outside of the city limits of Paris, which was theoretically against the law. A large group of college students would arouse suspicion and probably get the police involved, so they were cautious. Frederic reminded his mother:

> You know in Paris, as in Lyon, religious processions are prohibited, but ... there is no reason why we young Catholics should be deprived of one of the most moving ceremonies of our religion. Besides, some of us were determined to follow the procession at Nanterre ... the birthplace of the gentle Saint Genevieve.[115] [Saint Genevieve of the fifth century is the patron of Paris, whose relics had been desecrated during revolutionary activities.]

The collegians walked in procession with the parishioners of Nanterre, following the canopy—the priest holding the monstrance with the Blessed Sacrament. Frederic wrote,

> It was a pleasure to walk arm and arm with these fine people, to sing with them, and to see their naïve astonishment at our fine appearance and our piety! The procession was numerous, and the decorations full of simple elegance. All the homes were decorated and the roads were covered with flowers. The faith and piety that we beheld ... would be difficult to describe. The ceremony lasted nearly two hours. Then we attended High Mass where the crowd overflowed through the open doors of the church into the street. [116]

---

115 Letter, #58, his mother, 19 June 1833, Paris
116 Ibid.

Frederic Ozanam wrote about attending the celebration of the Mass at various places on special feast days at Notre Dame Cathedral, Paris. He also attended daily Mass as often as it was possible for him.

After he was forced to retire from active teaching, he and his wife Amelie, health permitting, would walk to Mass wherever they were. In Italy, he talked about the wonderful surprise of seeing so many of the common people at daily Mass.

> The altars here are attended even on week-days ... by artisans, coach drivers, peasants, and women who work in the markets, with whom you must rub shoulders, if you wish to sit on the benches, which take the place of our chairs. I attend eleven o'clock Mass nearly every day ... Holy Communions are more numerous than I expected.[117]

> You would not believe in what company I often find myself at the eleven o'clock Mass ... every class ... yet the poor whom the Savior loved.[118]

Frederic asked his priest brother Alphonse to celebrate seventeen Masses for the repose of the souls of family and friends and gave him the current stipend at the time. Frederic's intentions were for their father and mother, their sister Eliza, his father-in-law and brother-in-law Theophile, their grandparents and those of Amelie, for Andre-Marie Ampere, and for friends.

The saints, like Saint Teresa Benedicta of the Cross, teach that in order to penetrate our human life with the divine life, we must be in daily contact with God. Just as our earthly body needs its daily bread, so must our divine life be constantly fed.

---

117 Letter, #1232, Theophile Foisset, 4 February 1853, Pisa, Italy
118 Letter, #1245, Charles Benoit, 28 February 1853, Pisa, Italy

Frederic Ozanam understood this. From his boyhood days, he cultivated the habit of reading the Bible for thirty minutes every morning, He generally read sacred Scripture in Greek from an old edition that he particularly liked and marked the verses that struck him. Frederic called this his "daily bread."

The historical Jesus says, "Truly I tell you, just as you did it to one of the least of these who are members of my family (these, my brothers), you did it to me" (Matthew 25:40). Frederic Ozanam's patron Saint Vincent de Paul quoted this verse often in his presentations.

The twenty-three-year-old Frederic, however, took this thought to another level. He wrote Louis Janmot, one of his companions in the First Communion class,

> Both men and the poor we see with the eyes of the flesh; they are there and we can put finger and hand in their wounds and the scars of the crown of thorns are visible on their foreheads; and at this point incredulity no longer has place and we should fall at their feet and say with the Apostle, *Tu es Dominus et Deus meus* [My Lord and my God]. You are our masters, and we will be your servants. You are for us the sacred images of that God who we do not see, and not knowing how to love him otherwise shall we not love him in your persons?[119]

According to Frederic Ozanam, it is the risen Jesus whom we see in the poor. We touch their wounds and see their scars, which are his, our Lord and our God. We see the risen Jesus with eyes of the flesh, with the eyes of faith. The risen Jesus lives in the

---

119 Letter, #137, Louis Janmot, 13 November 1836, Lyon. Janmot was the artist who painted two portraits of Ozanam, one when he was twenty years old and the other at forty.

least of our brothers and sisters. To Father Tommaso Pendola, headmaster of a boys' school, Frederic wrote,

> You have among your children many who are rich, Reverend Father, oh! what a salutary lesson, how strengthening for those soft young hearts, to show them the poor, to show them Jesus Christ, not in pictures painted by great masters, or on altars resplendent with gold and light, but to show them Jesus Christ and his wounds in the person of the poor![120]

Previously, Frederic had written, "How much charity, devotion, and patience do we not need at present to heal the sufferings of these poor people, poorer than ever, because they have rejected the nourishment of the soul at the same time the bread of the body was lacking to them."[121] For Frederic, nourishment of soul would certainly include the Eucharist and the Word of God.

From his earliest days, confession was part of Frederic's spiritual regiment. The seventeen-year-old Frederic spoke about confession to his friend Auguste Materne,

> As to my religious duties, I make every effort to fulfill them exactly, especially confession, precisely because it costs me more. You would not believe how difficult it is for me to go to confession. My sloth complains, my pride groans, my scruples revive, I suffer. May God be understanding. I would put it off, but the more I put it off, the greater the pain. So I take the best remedy, which is promptness, and with the frequent repetition of the act, the less I have to tell, which bothers me less.[122]

---

120 Letter, #1319, Father Tommaso Pendola, 9 July 1853, Antignano, Italy

121 Letter, #137, Louis Janmot, 13 November 1836, Lyon

122 Letter, #13, Auguste Materne, 8 June 1830, Lyon

Mary: The Other Woman

There was another woman in Frederic Ozanam's life: the Blessed Virgin Mary. She didn't appear in his devotion during his adult years; she had been there his entire life.

A professor at Frederic's secondary school, the College Royal of Lyon that Frederic attended during the years 1823–1829, Mr. Urban Legeay, author *Of a Short Life* on Frederic Ozanam, secured the majority of Frederic's childhood poems because he saw in them, even at that early age, someone with remarkable literary ability.

In 1826, at thirteen years of age, Frederic composed a lengthy poem in honor of Mary completely in Latin, "Regina claris sideribus nitens" ("Queen shining in bright heavens"). The alcaic verses reflect the tender love and faithful trust that Frederic bore for Mary at the beginning of his teens. The evocation of the Immaculate Virgin without doubt is Notre-Dame de Fourviere.[123]

While Frederic does not intend to elaborate a Mariology, his letters express his undying devotion, love, and respect for Mary. This is evidenced partially by the number of Marian shrines that he and his wife would visit during their married life. Yet the shrine of Our Lady in the beautiful Fourviere basilica overlooking the magnificent city of Lyon was his first and last love.

The city of Lyon is known as "the city of martyrs," and Fourviere is known as "the hill that prays" because it was the site of the martyrs who were killed during the Roman persecution and because it is the location of several convents, the palace of the archbishop of Lyon, and the Basilica of Notre Dame de Fourviere.

---

123 Disquisitio, p.74. Comments are based on remarks of Urban Legeay "Ode Regina claris sideribus nitens du Serviteur de Dieu, 1826. This quotation is found also in Alphonse Ozanam's biography of his brother.

The name Fourviere finds its derivation from the Latin "forum vetus" ("old forum").[124] The Marian shrine occupies the site of the ancient Roman forum of Trajan.

Notre-Dame de Fourviere is accredited with the ending of the plague of 1643 and of preserving the city of Lyon during the cholera epidemics of 1832, 1835, and 1850, the latter three occurring during the lifetime of Frederic Ozanam. While Lyonnais citizens were fleeing the city and its environs because of the sweeping cholera, there was a band of people praying to Notre Dame at the shrine, asking for her intercession to save their city from devastating death. And the belief is that Notre Dame did intercede for Lyon.[125]

In a report to the general assembly of the Society of Saint Vincent de Paul, Frederic said, "Without doubt, our city (Lyon) is Catholic, the blood of its martyrs is alive, and the top of the venerated Basilica of Fourviere, the very holy Virgin Mary, surrounds it with a special protection."[126]

Frederic told friends that he knelt at Our Lady's altar over the years and made resolutions, one of which, we presume, was to live a better life and do a little good—his personal motto in life.

There were two other Marian shrines that were significant in Frederic Ozanam's spiritual life: Saint Mary the Greater in Burgos, Spain, and Notre Dame de Buglose, France. The Ozanams visited both these locations in the last years of Frederic's life.

Frederic, Amelie, and Marie arrived in Burgos, Spain, the evening of 18 November 1852, after a grueling thirty-three hours on the road. At the main altarpiece in the Cathedral of Burgos, before the niche of Saint Mary the Greater, Frederic had a lasting spiritual experience. He wrote about his trip in great detail in his

---

124 The French "Fourviere" finds its etymology in two Latin words.

125 Letter, #104, Francois Lallier, 23 September 1835, Villefranche, pres Lyon

126 Report as found in Letter #1360: General Assembly of the Society of St. Vincent de Paul, Lyon

work *Un Pelerinage au pays du Cid* ("A Pilgrimage in the Country of the Cid").

In the body of a letter to his brother Charles, Frederic wrote that he prayed to Mary,

> Ah! Holy Virgin, my mother, you are a powerful woman! And in return for your poor house of Nazareth, your divine Son has made you admirable houses. I am well acquainted with the beautiful ones from Our Lady of Cologne to Saint Mary Major, and from Saint Mary of Florence to Our Lady of Chartres. Here, the Spaniards ... have put aside their swords and have become masons in order to have a dwelling place for you among them. Good Virgin, who has obtained these miracles, obtain also something for us and for ours. Strengthen this fragile house and our dilapidated body; raise up to heaven the spiritual edifice of our souls.[127]

Notre Dame de Buglose is situated close to the birthplace of Saint Vincent de Paul, the berceau. Saint Vincent himself had prayed there.

Frederic told Francois Lallier that he went to confession to a Vincentian priest at Buglose, a man whose simplicity and extreme charity reminded him absolutely of their good patron, Saint Vincent de Paul. This excellent priest, Frederic continued, spoke to him about suffering patiently and of resignation and submission to God's will. This surprised Frederic because he was feeling quite well at the time. Frederic kept this fervorino in his heart for some time. The family had visited the shrine on 3 December 1852, and Frederic was still talking about the situation in a letter of 28 March 1853 to his close friend, Francois Lallier.

---

127 Letter, # 1197, Charles Ozanam, 18-19 November 1852, Burgos, Spain

On the Feast of the Assumption of Mary on 15 August 1853, Frederic attended Mass and received Holy Communion. Although he was extremely weak, he absolutely insisted on attending Mass. The Assumption meant special things to him: It was a special feast of the Blessed Mother, it was his deceased mother's feast when the entire family once had gathered in Lyon to be with her and enjoy a meal together, it was now the special day for his daughter Marie, and it was the day after Amelie's birthday. The Assumption would prove to be his last public Mass; the last time he would be able to physically walk even with assistance from Amelie.

Frederic died in less than a month on 8 September 1853, the Feast of the Birthday of Mary. How appropriate that God would honor such a man who had such devotion to Mary by taking him home on her birthday. Mary's natal day became Frederic's natal day into eternal life.

Saint Vincent de Paul: A Few Insights

What attracted Frederic Ozanam to Saint Vincent de Paul? What attracts anyone to Saint Vincent de Paul to be his follower? His normalcy as a human being? His ability to blend in with ordinary life and faith even in times of chaos and turmoil? His authentic concern for people in need? His unconditional and overarching love for people? His totally unselfish nature? His genuine love for God? Because what you saw was what you got?

Saint Vincent de Paul was no miracle worker—that is, he was not known as a person who performed wondrous unexplainable feats in order to meet a pressing need or to heal someone on the brink of serious danger or death. Vincent fed thousands of the destitute and refugees not by miracles but by organized teamwork. He rescued hundreds of abandoned babies by motivating others to come to their rescue. He drew people from all societal and economic levels and vocations, and they, in turn, worked collaboratively on projects. He succeeded where others did not. He got women out of the cloister and into active parish ministry after a stoppage of some six hundred years.

Saint Vincent de Paul disappears behind his amazing accomplishments, which, in some sense, were indeed miraculous. They fall under two principal areas: the alleviation of poverty and the reformation of priesthood.

If Vincent de Paul was to be promoted today for canonization, his cause could be advanced and substantiated by demonstrating how he practiced the theological and cardinal virtues to a heroic degree. The fact reminds that no one is ever beatified or canonized in the Catholic church because of achievements, however great or numerous. One is canonized because of one's holiness of life.

Vincent's holiness came about through his prayer life and his ministry, especially in the two areas of the poor and the priest. The poor gravitated to him because they sensed his genuine love and concern for them; the priests took to him because they sensed his love for him personally and for his priestly vocation.

Perhaps what others sense in followers of Saint Vincent de Paul is their genuineness and authenticity of purpose.

Saint Vincent de Paul: The Star

The magi followed a star and found Jesus. Is Saint Vincent de Paul a star? To whom does he lead?

There is a painting of Saint Vincent de Paul against a background of stars that depicts Vincent with three poor children. The painting is in possession of Fr. Greg Walsh, CM, in Australia. The painting is called *Vincent de Paul—Starry Night*. Frederic Ozanam wrote to his close friend, Francois Lallier,

> The star of Saint Vincent de Paul, raised much later on the horizon, is not destined, surely, to accomplish a shorter career. Let us work in his light. Let us honor our father in this patron so worthy of love, and we shall live long. We shall perhaps see one day the children of our old age find ample shade under this institution whose frail beginnings we have seen ... around us will rise, ever increasing, the flow of the Catholic generation, and we behold the time when we will overflow to inundate and renew the face of our poor country.[128]

Frederic Ozanam did not just know facts and quotes about Saint Vincent de Paul, he also knew the man, the saint. Frederic knew Vincent in a fashion and a language that even those priests and brothers of the saint's community do not commonly know him. To Frederic, Vincent was patron, father, star, and protector, to name but four delineating differences.

---

128 Letter, #175, Francois Lallier, 17 May 1838, Lyon

From where did Frederic obtain his knowledge of Vincent de Paul? From Emmanuel Bailly? From Sister Rosalie Rendu and her Daughter of Charity? Most probably the answer is yes. But other sources must not be forgotten. Frederic was a scholar par excellence; he no doubt read anything and everything available in French on this hero of France, who was then called Apostle of Charity and Father of the Poor.

In a letter to Francois Lallier, Frederic informs him, "We are reading now in place of the Imitation of Christ, the Life of Saint Vincent de Paul, to better penetrate ourselves with his example and traditions."[129]

Another source of Frederic's personal knowledge of Vincent de Paul was prayer. This is where knowledge converts into personal relationship, an abiding friendship. A sweep of Frederic's letters shows how often he referred to the saint, as there was an increase of references and citations to examples. Vincent was more than merely a figure from the past. He was a living presence. Frederic obviously had given this much thought and reflection:

A patron saint ... is a model one must strive to imitate, as he imitated the model of Jesus Christ. He is a life to be carried on, a heart in which one's own heart is enkindled, an intelligence from which light should be sought; he is a model on earth and a protector in heaven. A two-fold devotion is owed him: imitation and invocation. It is under these conditions only, of appropriating the thoughts and virtues of the saint that the Society can escape from the personal imperfections of its members, that it can make itself useful in the church and give reason for its existence.[130]

---

129 Ibid.

130 Ibid.

Saint Vincent de Paul, one of the most recently canonized saints (1737), has an immense advantage by reason of the nearness of the time when he lived, the infinite variety of benefits he bestowed, and the universality of admiration he inspires. The great souls who draw closest to God assume something of the gift of prophecy. Without doubt, Saint Vincent de Paul had an anticipated vision of the evils and the needs of our times. He was not a man to build on sand, nor for the moment.[131]

Members of the Society of Saint Vincent de Paul held general meetings four times a year; one of the dates was the Feast of Saint Vincent de Paul on 19 July (the feast is now 27 September, the day of the saint's death). The membership at times gathered for the celebration of Mass and prayer at the former parish where Vincent had been pastor—Clichy—or at the chapel of Saint Vincent de Paul, the maison-mere of the Vincentian community. Frederic has written about these occasions, his participation in the ceremonies, and in veneration of the relics of the saint.

At one such general meeting of the Society, Frederic praised Vincent and contrasted him with a giant of France's past, Cardinal Richelieu.

Richelieu was but a man of one country, of one period, of a few years. Saint Vincent de Paul is, on the other hand, for all lands and for all time. His name is celebrated wherever the sun illumines the crucifix on a church tower. His spirit visits the hospitals and schools of our faubourgs in the persons of his Sisters, as well as the Missions of Lebanon, China, and Texas, which are manned with his sons. His work never grows old: who does not wish today to continue

---

131 Ibid.

it? If we have courage and faith, gentlemen, what will keep us back?[132]

We shall be all together under the eyes of Saint Vincent de Paul our father, of the Blessed Virgin our mother, and of Jesus Christ our God.[133]

---

132 Frederic Ozanam, Cahiers Ozanam, Mary Ann Garry Hess, trans., Nos. 37/38/39 (January/June 1974): p.125

133 Disquisitio, op. cit., p.366, Second Report to the General Assembly, 17 July 1837. See Letter #157, Auguste La Taillandier, 21 August 1837 where Ozanam uses the same ending to his letter. In another Report to a General Assembly, 8 December 1836, Ozanam says: "France, which is the native land of Saint Vincent de Paul, the consecrated land to Mary, the eldest daughter of the Church of Jesus Christ." In a Letter #1367, 17 July 1837, Ozanam calls "Vincent de Paul our father, Holy Virgin Mary our queen, and Jesus Christ our God."

Saint Anthony of the Desert

The second letter extant from the pen of Frederic Ozanam is one to his "Cher Papa."

It was the major feast for his father and for himself, as the first name for both was Antoine. They considered Saint Anthony of the Desert as their patron saint, whose feast is celebrated on 17 January. The six-year-old Frederic wrote,

> I want to wish that the day of Saint Anthony will be a day of pleasure since it is your feast, I don't know how to make it better to celebrate, I can't give you more than a great deal of kisses and repeat it a thousand and a thousand times: I wish you a good feast; I will pray to Saint Anthony, who is a little of my friends, since it is my patron, of asking God that he conserve you a long life, a good health and I am with respect
>
> Your respectful son,
>
> Frederic Ozanam[134]

Saint Anthony lived in North Africa from 251 to 356 AD. The world is indebted to Saint Athanasius for his biography. Anthony was the prototype of Saint John the Baptist. Anthony sold all his possessions, including property, and went deep into the desert region of Egypt to spend his life in solitude, prayer, and

---

134 Letter, #2, to Frederic's father, 17 January 1820, Lyon. Frederic's first letter also was written to his father, 24 June 1819, the Feast of St. John the Baptist, who Frederic mentions, and tells his father that he loves him with all his heart.

mortification. We learn that Satan sent wild beasts to terrify him and appeared in strange configurations to frighten and actually attack him physically. Anthony clutched his rosary and held his ground. After many years of solitary living and due to his reputation for holiness, people started to search him out for advice and prayer requests.

At fifty-five, Anthony founded a community of monks who lived as hermits but came together for communal prayer, liturgy, and formation. Anthony died at the age of 105.

In a letter to his mother, Frederic wrote,

> Oh, how I feel attached to all the life of the family and how little I have of the solitary temperament of my patron Saint Anthony! Still the saint had an occasional companion of a living creature. My pen running on my paper is the only companion that I have, and that companion is often very sullen. Don't have any fear; I will not delay my return to you.[135]

Later in life, Frederic remembered his annual feast day in correspondence with other family members. In a letter to his priest brother Alphonse, he wrote, "One-thousand thanks for your good remembrance of Saint Anthony. I have been all the more touched that it's you who remember first and who so recalls my feast before the others."[136]

135 Letter, #146, to his mother, Tuesday, 11 April 1837, Paris

136 Letter, #776, Alphonse Ozanam, 19 January, 1848, Paris

Pauline Jaricot: Lay Apostle

Pauline Marie Jaricot was born in Lyon on 22 July 1799, ten years after the dreaded French Revolution, and died there in obscurity and poverty on 9 January 1862, almost three years after the death of her fellow Lyonnais Frederic Ozanam. The vivacious and attractive teen became pretty much the "it girl" of her day with involvement in the social life of the rich and famous of Lyon, but a fall in October of 1814 left her partially paralyzed and in severe pain. In addition, her mother died shortly afterward. It took months of rehabilitation for Pauline to recover emotionally and physically, but when she did, she resumed the social roller-coaster ride.

A Lenten sermon by Abbé Wurtz in 1816 derailed her express train. Pauline took the priest as her spiritual director, and boyfriends, romance novels, love songs, and the latest fashions went out the window. Pauline went from selfish to selfless. The transformation never stopped.

Her vocation became clear: a lay apostle in nineteenth century Lyon, France. Pauline committed herself to a life of prayer and deep devotion to our Lord in the Blessed Sacrament and received Holy Communion daily. She sold her jewelry and other things of value and shared the proceeds with the poor "who honor us by receiving us."

As a teenager, Pauline had a desire to help the missions in China and the United States, a desire no doubt fanned by her brother Phileas who was preparing for priesthood and often told her about the missionaries, their ministry, and his own desire to be a Chinese missionary. Pauline's desire to help the missions soon became her vocation.

In 1817, the eighteen-year-old organized the first collection for the Chinese missions. Two years later, she gathered workers in her family's factory into "circles of ten." Everyone in the group pledged to pray daily for the missions and missionaries and to give a penny. Each member of the group found ten friends to do the same. In spite of opposition from parish priests, Pauline refused to back down. She was a determined young woman.

The mission-minded group went from five hundred to one thousand in 1820. Their collection was sent to the Chinese missions via the Paris Foreign Mission Society. Pauline hoped to expand the distribution of funds to other missionary territory as well. In God's plan, in 1822, the Society for the Propagation of the Faith was born, of which the mission areas in Louisiana and Kentucky were recipients of assistance.

In a project on behalf of the working class, Pauline fell into debt. In spite of her success with the Society for the Propagation of Faith and later the Association of the Living Rosary, her life was one of the cross. She suffered on every front.

The famous cure of Ars, Saint Jean-Marie Vianney, was Pauline's spiritual director for many years. He said, "I know someone who knows how to accept the cross, and a heavy cross, and how to bear it with love! It is Miss Jaricot."[137]

The cure led pilgrimages from his small village of Ars to Notre-Dame-de-Fourviere in Lyon where Pauline lived and where Frederic Ozanam grew up under the loving care of his parents. Frederic entered the College Royal of Lyon in 1822, the same year Pauline launched her Society of the Propagation of the Faith.

Frederic took over as editor of the *Annals of the Propagation of the Faith* in 1838, which were published in Lyon. Not only did

---

137 Saint Jean-Marie Vianney, the famous Cure of Ars, at one time was a priest of the Archdiocese of Lyon. He often travelled to Lyon to buy liturgical vestments and other items for his parish. The saint became acquainted with Jaricot who was highly active in the archdiocese.

Frederic serve as editor, he also wrote articles on various subjects pertinent to the missionary nature of the church. In one article, he wrote,

> The fault of many Christians of our days is they hope little. It's each combat, it's each obstacle, to believe the ruin of the church. They are the apostles in the boat during the storm: they forget that the Savior is in the midst of them; they forget that all ages of the church have had plenty of perils in order that it should fear, but also plenty of help for it should hope. Catholicism, which in our days still has its storms, also has its reassuring signs. The work of the Propagation, in doing with so little means so many things, in showing to Catholics what they can for unity, in showing them all the dedication in the priesthood, in religious communities, in neophytes of distant Christian countries, in publicizing the victories of truth, serve admirably to renew courage.[138]

Frederic and Amelie Ozanam were married in the Church of Saint-Nizier, the location where the body of Pauline Jaricot is buried. Blessed Pope John XXIII proclaimed her venerable in 1963, and the cause for her beatification and canonization continues.

Frederic Ozanam's editorship of and authoring in the *Annals of the Propagation* was a great blessing in his life. He owed it in some sense to Pauline Marie Jaricot, his fellow Lyonnais.

---

138 Letter, #599 Dominique Meynis, 29 January 1845, Paris

Blessed Rosalie Rendu, DC

During the days of Frederic Ozanam in Paris, two other disciples of Saint Vincent de Paul were contemporaries of his. These were two Daughters of Charity of Saint Vincent de Paul whom we know today as Saint Catherine Laboure and Blessed Rosalie Rendu. Blessed Rosalie Rendu, DC, had the reputation that people now would attribute to a Blessed Mother Teresa of Calcutta, certainly in the Mouffetard district of Paris if not throughout the entire "City of Light." Sister Rosalie was a woman of passion, phenomenal organizational ability, and holiness of life.

She was fearless, living and ministering in an area of Paris that she called her diocese but one that teemed with danger. Sister Rosalie often defended the area:

> It is calumny; [the quarter] is far better than its reputation; its poverty reveals less depravity and malice than many rich quarters conceal under their luxury and wealth.[139]

She oozed courage; no one, at any level, intimidated her, except her God. During the plagues that killed hundreds in her area, she walked the streets and collected the dead. During the revolutionary combats, she mounted the barricades and literally stopped the fighting to remove the dead and wounded from both sides.

In a well-documented case, a new police commissioner announced to his men that he was going to arrest Sister Rosalie

---

139 Armand du Melun, Vie de la soeur Rosalie Rendu, Fille de la Charite, 13th edition, pp.153-154, Paris, 1929. See also Sister Rosalie Rendu: A Daughter of Charity on Fire with Love of the Poor, Sister Louise Sullivan, D.C., Vincentian Studies Institute, Chicago, p.331.

for caring for the wounded rebels. His subordinates refused to accompany him. Their reason: "You will never come out alive!" The police who walked the beats knew the unbounded love that the "dangerous poor" had for Sister. If the ordinary person would think twice before ever walking in Mouffetard even in broad daylight, what authority figure would dare threaten to remove the one hope of the poor, their one genuine source of assistance, their bond to survival? That person would be jeopardizing one's existence! Incidentally, the police commissioner did see Sister Rosalie, slapped her on the wrist at most, but in reality she completely disarmed him. He walked away with more humility than he had previously.

Persons of every rank and file came to Sister Rosalie for advice and counsel. This included everyone from the Catholic hierarchy to top government officials, from the single pregnant woman to the man starving to death. Each person lined up and took his or her turn; there were no exceptions. When Sister Rosalie received the highest honor from the French government, Napoleon III came to her office. She did not go to his palace.

Rosalie was not a Lone Ranger. She had a network of relationships and, because of her organizational skills, knew how to use and did use others in ministry for the good of others. Collaboration was one of her fortes.

Sister Rosalie's burning passion to serve the destitute and anyone in need drove her to embrace what we might call "the seamless garment" approach. She was vitally concerned for every age of life: the newborn, the child, the teen, and the adult. As a consequence, Rosalie initiated programs to address the issues involved at the respective level, e.g., infant care, education of children, support of the elderly, supervision of young working girls, and service of the poor in their homes. Her ministry involved not only acts of charity but also strived in the area of systemic change.

Frederic Ozanam and Sister Rosalie became acquainted after she was well established in the Mouffetard district of Paris. At the recommendation of Mr. Emmanuel Bailly, the president of the newly founded Society of Saint Vincent de Paul, the first members of the organization contacted Sister Rosalie for her assistance in how to work with the poor and for a list of people to see.

Bailly and his wife knew Sister Rosalie well and had been involved in some of her programs. As the Sorbonne was in easy walking distance to Sister Rosalie's residence, it was convenient for the students to see her. Rosalie liked what she saw in these original six of the Society of Saint Vincent de Paul and what they had in mind: doing hands-on ministry with God's poor. They were in and stayed in.

She divided them into twos because Jesus sent his seventy-two disciples out in twos; besides, that is the way the Daughters of Charity visited the homes of the poor – two Sisters at a time. They believed what Jesus said, "For where two or three are gathered in my name, I am there among them" (Matthew 18:20). For Sister Rosalie and her religious community, their home visits always meant three— Jesus was with the two Sisters. That is the way the first members of the Society saw it: Jesus was with the two collegians.

Sister Rosalie explained to them how to use vouchers for bread and coal, offered them supervision, and gave advice that is as good today as it was then,

After death in February 1856, the Council General of the Society of St. Vincent de Paul wrote of Sister Rosalie:

> She was one of the principal instruments whom Providence served to assist and develop the conferences of St. Vincent de Paul.[140]

---

140 Disquisitio, op. cit., p.313

Frederic Says Goodbye

To Family and Friends

Frederic Says Good-Bye

Frederic Ozanam resigned as a member of the faculty at the Sorbonne. It was a difficult decision, but he was forced to do so by reason of health issues. He gave his last lectures in April 1852. Frederic's health was precarious at best since his brush with typhoid fever at seven years of age. From that time on, his physical condition was described as delicate and fragile. He seemed to be quite susceptible to respiratory problems.

When he felt up to it, he and Amelie would walk to daily Mass at the Church of Saint Joseph des Carmes near their home. That house no longer exists, and the church is now located on the property of the Institut Catholique of Paris, which did not exist in Frederic's day.

One morning, in spite of Frederic having a fever, he and Amelie entered the church, and she knelt behind him. She did not want the love of her life to see her tears. She felt deep inside that he would never recover. The medical profession did not have the know-how or wherewith to cure Bright's disease.[141]

As Mass was about to conclude, Amelie knew that she had to brighten up and stop crying. She looked at the side altar, one in honor of the guardian angels. There on the left wall, she saw a plaque written in French, "Here rests Antoine-Frederic Ozanam." She would swear to her dying day that she saw those words.

During his adult years after marriage, Frederic appeared to have been conscientious in maintaining his health. The Ozanams spent

---

141 In French, the medical condition had been referred to as "maladie de Breglet." At least, this is what Frederic calls it in a letter dated 30 April 1853 to his priest-brother, Alphonse. The malady is named after the London medical doctor Richard Bright (1789-1858).

their free time at health spas or in areas near and far from Paris: the sea air and baths at Saint-Gildas-de-Rhuys, Dieppe, Sceaux, the waters at Eaux-Bonnes, and the sea air at Saint Biarritz. One moment Frederic's strength would be stabilized or improved, the next moment he would be weak and washed out. Bright's disease was entrenching itself in his body. In the long haul, he would show some stamina until the last weeks of his life.

This was reminiscent of Jesus' way of the cross—wherein weakened by beatings and the loss of blood, hunger, and dehydration, Jesus carried a heavy wooden crossbeam on his way to death. Jesus fell, got up; fell, got up, and kept moving forward. Along the way, Jesus needed help carrying the instrument of crucifixion and found it in the person of Simon of Cyrene.

In spite of Frederic's various illnesses and his ups and downs, he continued forward; he knew that his Calvary was in sight. He had assistance along his way of the cross: his wife Amelie; his brothers, especially Charles the doctor; and members of the Society of Saint Vincent de Paul.

Easter 1852 was not a time of resurrection for Frederic; he was more in the death cycle of the paschal mystery. Almost immediately after Mass at Notre Dame, Frederic came down with a fever and was forced to bed. He tells us that he was at death's door with pleurisy. His brother Charles came to the rescue combined with "the care of my family, the prayers of my friends, and the mercy of God."[142]

Some weeks later, he regained some strength and was determined to travel to Eaux-Bonnes. Because of the long distance involved, the Ozanams broke up the journey into short spurts. From Eaux-Bonnes, the family went to enjoy the sea baths at Biarritz. Frederic's intention was to spend the winter in the south of France.

---

142 Letter, #1130, Louis Harabeder, 11 April 1852 (Easter Sunday), Paris,

In a letter to his friend, the future bishop Henri Maret, Frederic said that whether God's design for him was to regain his health or to make him do reparation for his sins by prolonged suffering, may God be equally praised and blessed. Let God only give "me the courage and send me the suffering that purifies. May my cross be that of the penitent thief." And Frederic asked Father Maret to remember him in his prayers.[143]

Biarritz proved to be a good place for Frederic. His brother Charles's presence for three weeks certainly was helpful. Frederic realized that he needed more strength before he could ever consider himself cured.

Frederic was too close to the Spanish border not to cross, and so he did. When he felt strong enough, the family traveled to San Sebastian. Although it was the end of October, the weather was like mid-July, a godsend. Although the trek into Spain tired him, Frederic went further to Burgos, where he had a moving experience before the statue of Our Lady in the cathedral. Revived, he seemed to have a new lease on life.

Crossing the Pyrenees back into France, there remained something important that Frederic had to do: visit the birthplace of Saint Vincent de Paul in the Dax area. One of the Vincentian priests gave Frederic cuttings from the historic oak tree dating from the time of Saint Vincent de Paul. These made a deep impression on Frederic, and he often shared his gift with others.

At the shrine of Our Lady of Buglose, a site where Saint Vincent de Paul himself had prayed as a young man, Frederic had another spiritual experience. Frederic went to confession to a Vincentian priest at the shrine, and the priest spoke only of sufferings to be endured patiently, of resignation, and submission to God's will, however that might be. This feverino surprised Frederic as a penitent, as he actually was feeling quite well at the time. The

---

143 Letter, #1171, Father Henri Maret, 14 September 1852, Biarritz

priest had no idea who Frederic was and certainly knew nothing about his physical condition. The priest's words turned out to have a prophetic ring to them. Frederic soon became weak again.

Family members supported the Ozanams along their journey, cousins in Provence, Toulon, Cannes, and Nice.

The Ozanams traveled to Marseille. Here, Amelie's parents were married; here, Amelie was born; here, the Soulacrix had relatives and friends. Christmas 1852 was a beautiful family celebration. Frederic and the family had to pay a visit to the great shrine of Notre-Dame-de-Gard overlooking the city, patroness and protector of Marseilles since the thirteenth century.

Poor Frederic came down with swollen feet, frequent painful muscles spasms, and dilation of the heart that he had had before and for which he had been treated with digitalis. "I hope that this little check will not last, and that God may send it to me as a New Year gift, so that I may say, 'I will how you will, I will when you will.'"[144] This was one of Frederic's favorite spiritual sayings from *The Imitation of Christ*.

Where to spend winter? Bayonne, Spain, or Italy? The Ozanams chose Italy, the country of Frederic's birth.

The Ozanam family boarded the *Marie Antoinette* in Genoa. The crossing was rough, and the rain bordered on torrential. They docked at Pisa on 10 January 1853 and headed directly to the cathedral. Frederic felt relieved; the family could finally settle down after concluding an excessive amount of traveling. His hope was to regain his strength in Italy.

Frederic could never just rest and relax as he was instructed

---

144 Letter, #1219, Charles Ozanam, 2 January 1853, Nice. Ozanam prayed this phrase in several letters, e.g., to Charles Benoit from Biarritiz, France, 3 November 1852, to Dr. Salvat Franchisteguy from Pisa, Italy, 3 April 1853. As the members of the Society of St. Vincent de Paul at one time read sections of *The Imitation of Christ* during their meetings, Ozanam could have selected the prayer from those days, or did he adapt the prayer from Pope Clement XI (1700-1721) who often quoted it during his pontificate?

to do. He continued to write and visit conferences of the Society of Saint Vincent de Paul wherever he was in southern France and Spain, and he would do the same in Italy. And if the Society was not in a certain location, Frederic would do everything in his power to have a conference of the Society established. The Society was his family. Besides, God's poor needed assistance, and Frederic's desire was that they receive it.

A case in point: Tuscany. There was no Society of Saint Vincent de Paul there because of political reasons more than anything else. So Frederic played a major role in establishing a conference there. His reputation as a scholar of Dante in the land of Dante certainly worked in his favor as he worked out details with the authorities. To his delight, the Society received official authorization in Florence, Pisa, and Livorno. But Frederic wrote to his friend Theophile Foisset,

> My health is almost altogether gone. May it please heaven to deliver me. So many prayers cannot remain unheard; but it seems also that my sins cannot remain unpunished.
>
> Since I left France, the fatigue of traveling has broken my strength, and I am suffering, tottering, but without falling, almost like the leaning tower before which I pass daily. That example should reassure and instruct me; for leaning as it is, it has not ceased during some seven hundred years to serve God in its own way, by celebrating him with the chime of its bells.[145]

Amelie laid down the law and strove to enforce a tight daily schedule for Frederic. He got up at 9:00 a.m., ate breakfast close to the fire, attended Mass at 11:00 a.m. if his stamina was good

---

145 Letter, #1232, Theophile Foisset, 4 February 1853, Pisa

enough to walk to the church, read in the nearby library, returned to the house to write a letter or give a lesson to daughter Marie, ate dinner close to the fire, and went to bed after a little reading.[146]

Frederic had a plan: If God gave him the strength to do so, on his return to France, he would deliver several lectures on the poem "The Cid" that he had authored as a fruit of their trip to Spain.

The Ozanams traveled to Antignano, Italy, located south of Livorno on the western side of Tuscany, off the Mediterranean and Tyrrhenian Seas. Unknown to the Ozanams, Saint Elizabeth Ann Seton had been in the Livorno area some years before. She had brought her husband William there with the hope of recovering his health, but tuberculosis had won out.

On Montenero, in view of Livorno and Antignano, is the pilgrim shrine of Our Lady of Grace of Montenero, patron of Tuscany. There Elizabeth Ann Seton and the Ozanams prayed. Frederic wrote to his brother Charles,

> Montenero … we went there once. I could not think of climbing on foot this steep way. Carriages for getting up there cost very dear. Still we could not remain behind the good Christians of the country, who all go to make a visit there in the month of May. It is the Fourviere of Leghorn (Livorno), but a Fourviere all shining with marble, gilding, silver lamps, and magnificent votive offerings.
>
> Nevertheless, besides the gifts offered by the gratitude of the rich, we see with emotion the offerings of the poor … old clothes, crutches, and canes. Oh, how happy I would have been to hang my cane also in this sanctuary, and come down on foot, but I have not the lively faith which obtains miracles. The whole family, including Marie, took part

---

146 Letter, #1249. Father Henri Maret, 4 March 1853, Pisa

in the excursion, and came back with their hands full of pictures and medals, thanks to the kindness of the Father Abbot, who in his desire to give a good welcome to the Mr. Professor, and to make us admire his marble and lamps, left us scarcely time to say our rosary.[147]

In addition to his serious disease, Frederic was concerned about his finances and his ability to care for Amelie and Marie. He addressed this issue with his brother Charles as he did his physical troubles (Letter, 9 May 1853).

There was one bright spot in all of this. Little Marie began attending catechism classes. Frederic was as proud as a peacock. The parish priest asked her questions publicly, and the little "rascal" boldly repeated the Ten Commandments, the sacraments, and the act of contrition all in Italian![148]

But Frederic was extremely ill. He tells Dr. Salvat Franchisteguy,

> I know that my illness is serious, but I have not despaired; that it will take a long time to heal, and that I may not heal; but I force myself to abandon myself with love to the will of God, and I say—more with the lips than with my heart, I am afraid! *Volo quod vis, volo quamdiu vis, volo quia vis* (I will what you will, I will when you will, I will because you will).[149]

Members of the Society of Saint Vincent de Paul—"brothers"— would take turns sitting with Frederic at his bedside. They must have evoked memories of his mother's Society of Watchers. This

147 Letter, #1298, Charles Ozanam, 21-23 May 1853, Livourne, Italy

148 Ibid., written from San Jacopo, Italy, 22 May 1853

149 Letter, #1269, Dr. Salvat Franchisteguy, 3 April 1853, Pisa, Italy

served as a great help to Amelie; she could then give more attention to their daughter Marie and to her household chores. Amelie need not worry about her failing husband, as he was in good hands.

These members of the Society of Saint Vincent de Paul looked upon Frederic not in admiration for all his accomplishments as a renowned professor at the Sorbonne, but as one of the principal founders of their Society that had spread throughout the world from its humble beginning in Paris. They viewed him as a dear brother who loved the poor as they did and who had given hours upon hours of his life for those in dire need. They saw Frederic as one of their own who now was dying and preparing to meet his Creator.

Once, Frederic started to cry. One of the members of the Society asked him, "Why do you worry about yourself? Take it easy. You'll soon see France." Frederic answered, "My brother, it is not that. When I think of my sins, for which God has suffered so much, how can I refrain from tears?"[150]

Another time when he cried, one asked him, "Are you such a great sinner?" And he said, "Brother, you do not understand what the holiness of God is."[151]

Frederic spent his days in prayer and deep reflection. At Antignano, he spent much of the day on a sofa in the open air on the terrace of their rental on the Mediterranean Sea. Little Marie would occasionally come and ask him for a hug and then go off to her own world. She knew that her papa was sick and not to bother him too much.

Frederic had made an act of consecration to God. "Lord, you have lent me this body. No other sacrifice whatever could please you. Behold me then, I come, as it is written at the beginning of your book. It is your will that I shall do, my God."

Every day, Frederic prayed sacred Scripture for thirty minutes

---

150 Baunard, op.cit., p.400
151 Ibid.

after rising in the morning. He called it his "daily bread." Now he had a companion—the Bible, the only book that he read. It was his book of consolation as he wrestled with Bright's disease. During some of the day, he would isolate all verses having to do with sickness and healing, and Amelie would write down his comments.

One evening after Marie had been put to bed, the two of them were left alone. Frederic was lying on the sofa, admiring the sunset over the Mediterranean. Amelie deliberately was sitting behind him because she did not want Frederic to see her crying. One of the things that struck her was the serenity of her husband's face—the same look on the face of her brother Theophile before he died.

Amelie asked Frederic what was the greatest gift of God that he valued in his life. "In a flash, without any period of reflection, he said, 'Peace of heart; without it, no good can make us happy; with it, every trial, even the approach of death, can be endured."[152]

Frederic wrote an old friend,

> You can have no idea of the resources she (his guardian angel and wife Amelie) has discovered in her heart, not only to relieve but to cheer me; with what ingenious, patient, indefatigable tenderness she surrounds my life, guessing, anticipating every wish ... divine providence, while trying us, does not abandon us. God treats us mercifully; and if there are days of despondency, there are moments too of exquisite enjoyment between my wife and child.[153]

Charles Ozanam received a telegram. As a medical doctor, he knew that his brother's time was almost up, so he arrived on 15 August. Father Ozanam arrived shortly later. Frederic was definitely failing quickly, and there was no remedy for his disease.

---

152 O'Meara, op.cit., p.343

153 Letter, #1269, Dr. Salvat Franchisteguy, 3 April 1853, Pise, Italy

Frederic wanted to die on French soil; he wanted to go home. On 31 August, they booked passage on the *Industrie* and sailed from Livorno to Marseille. The ship docked on Friday, 2 September with 110 passengers aboard. Members of the family, including Amelie's mother, met the ship.

They rented a house and members of the Society of Saint Vincent de Paul came to pray and pay respects to a man most did not know but knew only by reputation. Frederic received the last rites of the church from the cure of the local parish and received Holy Communion with extraordinary fervor. Afterward, when the priest thought to calm Frederic's anxiety of his approaching death, Frederic immediately cut him short. "Why should I fear? I love him so much."[154]

On the morning of 8 September, the end was apparent, but Frederic persisted. Finally, at 7:15 p.m., in the presence of his wife and two brothers, he held out his arms and cried out in a loud voice, "My God, my God, have mercy on me!"[155] Those were his last words.

Father Alphonse Ozanam recited the prayers for the repose of Frederic's soul. It was Thursday, the Feast of the Birthday of the Blessed Virgin Mary whom he loved and to whom he had prayed all his life. Frederic was now with the other woman in his life.

The Ozanam family cemetery plot was in Lyon. Should Amelie Ozanam bury him there? But she wanted his body near her in Paris.

After his passing in Marseille, the body was transported to Lyon. There in Saint-Pierre's Church where his parents and family had worshipped for years and where Frederic had made his First Communion, a funeral Mass was celebrated for the sake of family,

---

154 O'Meara, op. cit., p.345. Father Lacordaire also mentions this instance in his biography of Ozanam, p.67.

155 Ibid.

friends, and members of the Society of Saint Vincent de Paul. People requested that Amelie leave Frederic's body in Lyon, and they would erect a monument for him at Loyasse Cemetery.

But Amelie said no. She refused to separate herself from her husband at a great distance, but she did seem to be open if the body could be interred in a church. She had read where the French government was thinking again of allowing burials in churches. It surfaced that the local authorities in Lyon were not yet open to church burials.

Frederic's body went to Paris. Another funeral Mass was held at the Church of Saint-Sulpice on 15 September 1853. After the ceremony, the coffin was placed next to the chapel of the Blessed Virgin. Church workers did not want to touch his body; the pastor asked that the coffin be removed as soon as possible.

Several family members suggested that Amelie bury Frederic in Montparnasse Cemetery to get it over with. There had been three funeral Masses; this was going on too long. Family members told her that she would not get what she wanted, but Amelie was persistent; she kept knocking on doors.

Amelie went to talk to the Dominicans, who were staffing Saint Joseph des Carmes, and, in God's providence, who was there but the Dominican provincial, Father Henri Lacordaire. He definitely wanted Frederic's remains brought to the Carmelite church. That was exactly what Amelie wanted to hear.

Permission was needed to transport the body from Saint Suplice to Saint Joseph. The Dominican found a spot carved out by agents of the massacre of September 1792. Frederic himself wanted to be buried there because he knew of those 114 priests who were murdered there. Between 2–3 September, 191 bishops and priests had been killed. To Amelie's amazement and joy, Frederic's tomb was located directly below the Chapel of the Guardian Angels where she had seen written on the wall, "Here rests Antoine-Frederic Ozanam."

At the end of 1855, Amelie traveled to Rome accompanied by her mother and daughter. They had an audience with Pope Blessed Pius IX, who remembered Frederic. He granted her permission to enter her husband's tomb through the Dominican residence.

Amelie made several other changes pertinent to the tomb, including a staircase. She had cut the following inscription:

> A. F. Ozanam, most pious and faithful interpreter of the universal truth and charity. He lived 40 years, 4 months and 16 days and died on 8 September 1853. Dedicated by Amelie to the spouse with whom she lived for twelve years and by Marie to her father. Live in God and pray for salvation.[156]

---

156 This is a translation of the Latin from Frederic Ozanam's tomb in Paris.

A Final Word on Family

Frederic Ozanam told Father Tommaso Pendola three months before his death,

> This dear Society [the Society of Saint Vincent de Paul] is also my family. It is, after God, what kept me in the faith, when I had lost my good and pious parents. I love it, and I hold it in the deepest part of my heart.

> We have conferences in Quebec and in Mexico. We are in Jerusalem. We have the same assurance of one conference in paradise, because more than one thousand of ours, since we have existed for twenty years, have taken the way of a better life.[157]

---

157 Letter, #1319, Father Tommaso Pendola, 9 July 1853, Antignano, Italy

Bibliography

I recommend the following materials on the life of Blessed Frederic Ozanam. I have relied on some of them for my sources in writing this book. Not all of them are available in English.

Sacra Congregatio pro Causis Sanctorum, Beatificationis et Canonizationis Servi Dei Frederici Ozanam. Disquisitio, Rome, 1980. French

Sacra Congregatio pro Causis Sanctorum, Positio Super Virtutibus. Informatio et Summarium, Rome, 1990. French

Lettres de Frederic Ozanam, Societe de Saint-Vincent-de-Paul, Paris. There are five volumes published over the years in French. While some of the letters have been translated into English and Spanish, many have not been.

Frederic Ozanam: A Life in Letters, translated and edited by Father Joseph I. Dirvin, C.M., Society of St. Vincent de Paul Council of the United States, St. Louis, Mo. 1986

Ozanam in His Correspondence, Msgr. Louis Baunard, Benziger Brothers, New York, 1925. This book was translated into English from the original French by an unnamed member of the Society of Saint Vincent de Paul, the Council of Ireland.

Frederic Ozanam: His Life and Works, Kathleen O'Meara, New York Christian Press Association Publishing Co., New York, 1911

The Great Friend: Frederic Ozanam, Albert Paul Schimberg, Bruce Publishing Company, Milwaukee, 1946

Memorial of the Beatification of Frederic Ozanam, various authors. Editions du Signe, Strasbourg, France, 1997. This booklet is beatifically photographed and contains excellent material.

Ozanam, various authors, Editions du Signe, Strasbourg, France, 1997. This author wrote co-authored a section of this magazine. As usual Editions du Signe has produced an extraordinary publication.

Praying with Frederic Ozanam, Ronald Ramson, C.M., St. Mary's Press, Christian Brothers Publications, Winona, Minnesota 1998. Translations in Spanish and Portuguese are available.

Apostle in a Top Hat, James Patrick Derum, Hanover House, 1960.

15 Days of Prayer with Blessed Frederic Ozanam, Christian Verheyde, translated John E. Rybolt, C.M., New City Press, 2013.

Ozanam, Madeleine Des Rivieres, translated James Parry, Les Editions Bellarmin, Montreal, 1989.

CPSIA information can be obtained at www.ICGtesting.com
Printed in the USA
LVOW08s1715021213

363571LV00001B/278/P